Guitar Essentials

787.87
aul

Published in 2001 by Silverdale Books
An imprint of Bookmart Ltd
Registered number 2372865
Trading as Bookmart Ltd
Desford Road
Enderby
Leicester LE19 4AD

Reprinted 2002
Copyright © 2001 De Agostini UK Ltd

ISBN 1-85605-598-1

This material previously appeared in the reference set *Play Guitar*

Produced by
Amber Books Ltd
Bradley's Close
74–77 White Lion Street
London N1 9PF
www.amberbooks.co.uk

Printed in Singapore

Guitar Essentials

Guitar Essentials is a practical guide to the techniques and fundamentals of guitar playing

CONTENTS

C18265

MIXING AND RECORDING

CHORDS AND NOTES

CLASSIC GUITARS

GET TO KNOW YOUR GUITAR

Electric and acoustic guitars both have a similar design, although the electric guitar needs to be connected to an amplifier for sound output.

Your choice of guitar depends largely on the type of music you want to play and the kind of sound you want to achieve. However, both instruments have the same basic design, and if you can play one, you can play the other.

Both are six-string instruments (a bass guitar, on the other hand, only has four strings) and have a body, neck and machine heads for tuning. The strings on both guitars are tuned to the same standard tuning. The strings pass through a 'bridge' on the body to the machine heads on the headstock. They are plucked or strummed with a finger or plectrum to produce sound.

The electric guitar is usually solid and has 'pick-ups' situated between the neck and the bridge. These convert the vibrations of the strings into electrical signals and send them to an external amplifier. The acoustic, in contrast, has a large, hollow sound-box, designed to amplify the vibrations of the strings naturally.

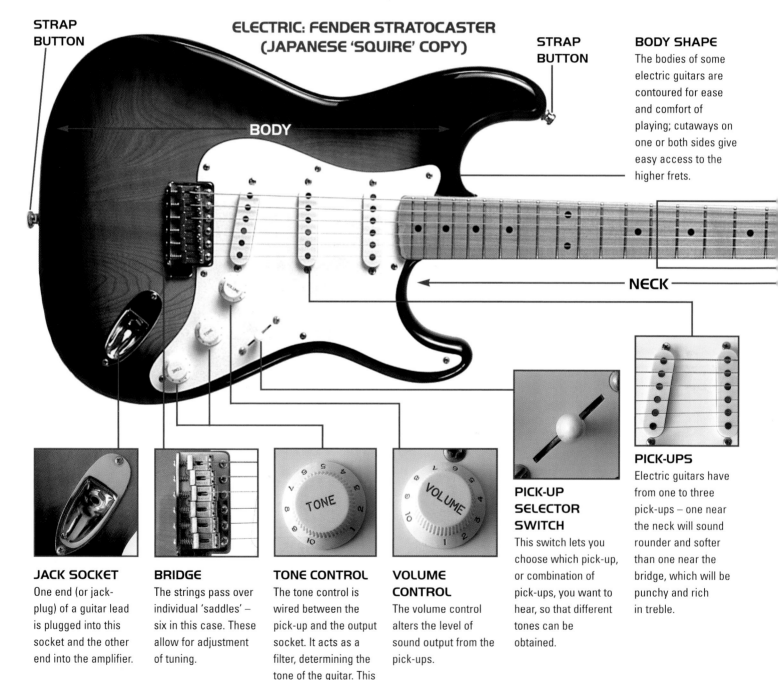

STRAP BUTTON

ELECTRIC: FENDER STRATOCASTER (JAPANESE 'SQUIRE' COPY)

STRAP BUTTON

BODY

NECK

BODY SHAPE
The bodies of some electric guitars are contoured for ease and comfort of playing; cutaways on one or both sides give easy access to the higher frets.

PICK-UPS
Electric guitars have from one to three pick-ups – one near the neck will sound rounder and softer than one near the bridge, which will be punchy and rich in treble.

JACK SOCKET
One end (or jack-plug) of a guitar lead is plugged into this socket and the other end into the amplifier.

BRIDGE
The strings pass over individual 'saddles' – six in this case. These allow for adjustment of tuning.

TONE CONTROL
The tone control is wired between the pick-up and the output socket. It acts as a filter, determining the tone of the guitar. This guitar has two tone controls.

VOLUME CONTROL
The volume control alters the level of sound output from the pick-ups.

PICK-UP SELECTOR SWITCH
This switch lets you choose which pick-up, or combination of pick-ups, you want to hear, so that different tones can be obtained.

Fretboard

The metal frets are hammered into notches in the fretboard. The fretboard is made of a hardwood such as maple (shown here) or rosewood, and glued onto the face of the neck. The number of frets varies: an acoustic tends to have 20, while an electric has 22 or 24. Only the first seven frets are shown below.

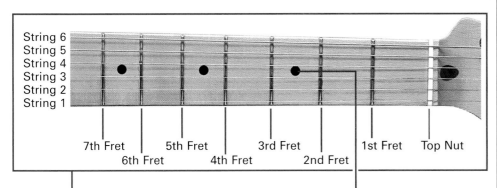

String 6
String 5
String 4
String 3
String 2
String 1

7th Fret   5th Fret   3rd Fret   1st Fret   Top Nut
    6th Fret   4th Fret   2nd Fret

Guitar Gear

Plectrums are used to strike the guitar strings. They can be made of plastic or nylon, and produce a strong, clear and even tone. Thin plectrums make fast strumming easier; thick plectrums create a harsher sound, which is good for 'power chords' and fast lead playing. While learning, use medium gauge plectrums; they're ideal for strumming and individual note picking. Nylon ones tend to break fewer strings, but really, you should choose the type that feels most comfortable.

DOT MARKERS
The dots set in the fretboard of some guitars are a handy visual guide to fret positions. They are usually found behind the 3rd, 5th, 7th, 9th and 12th frets, and often on the upper edge of the fretboard.

MACHINE HEADS
Turning the machine heads changes the tension of each string and its tuning. Some guitars have three machine heads on either side of the headstock; this Fender Stratocaster has all six on one side.

← **HEADSTOCK** →

MACHINE HEADS
Each side of the headstock of an acoustic guitar has three machine heads for tuning.

ACOUSTIC: TAKAMINE EN-10

SOUND HOLE
The opening lets the sound of the string be amplified by the hollow sound-box. It is often surrounded by a decorative rosette.

BRIDGE
The wooden bridge, firmly glued to the face of the guitar, has a bone or plastic 'saddle', which the strings pass over.

BODY SHAPE
Its curved shape makes the acoustic guitar comfortable to play when seated, letting it rest on your leg. The size and shape of the sound-box produces different tonal properties; the larger, wide-bottomed acoustics tend to have a more bass, booming sound and greater volume.

PLAYING BASICS

Before you start strumming, you need to work out the most comfortable and effective playing positions for your guitar, plectrum and fingers.

Sitting posture

It's a good idea to sit while you practice, as you'll be more relaxed. This will result in better technique and control. Rest the lower curve of the guitar body on your leg, with the neck pointing slightly upwards. Rest your right arm against the upper rim of the guitar, so that your hand is poised over the strings. Your left hand should be able to move freely along the neck, with the thumb behind the fretboard.

String facts

Guitar strings come in varying degrees of thickness. There's a reason for this: the thicker the string, the lower the note. A thick string will produce a deeper note than a thin string that's tuned to the same tension. Finger positioning also affects the pitch of a note. A note played at a fret near the body of the guitar is always higher in pitch than a note played on the same string at a fret that's closer to the headstock.

Buzzing or rattling strings could mean it's time to change them.

SOUNDBITE

WHEN TOP IS BOTTOM
String 6 is the thickest string at the top of your guitar. However, it is always referred to as the 'bottom' string because it plays the deepest note.

A guitar player's fingernails

All players should keep the nails of the left (fretting) hand quite short, to avoid catching the strings when changing chord positions. The right-hand (plucking) nails can also be kept short if you plan always to use a plectrum. Some players, however, use the nails of their plucking hand for 'finger-picking', and so need them to be long and tough. Steel strings are hard on nails, so a plectrum is an ideal option. Many players, such as Mark Knopfler of Dire Straits, just use their fingers; it's all down to personal preference – and the strength of your nails.

Finger tip

HOLDING A PLECTRUM
Perfect string picking begins with holding the plectrum correctly. The best way to control your plectrum is to hold it lightly between your right-hand thumb and index finger (top). Hold it close to the tip to control its movement, leaving only the pointed tip showing.

If you hold your plectrum too close to the wider edge and more of the plectrum is visible (bottom), you'll find that it will be difficult to handle and your strikes will be too loose to create a crisp, clean sound.

TUNING YOUR STRINGS

Tuning your guitar is essential before playing, as the strings need to be in harmony. You'll soon develop a 'feel' for the correct pitch.

There are three main aids to tuning: by tuning fork, electronic tuner or by pitch pipes.
Each open string should be adjusted to be in tune with the others. Start by plucking the 6th string, and keep it ringing as you turn the machine head, so you can hear the pitch change and recognize when the string is in tune. Repeat the process for each string.

Using the machine heads

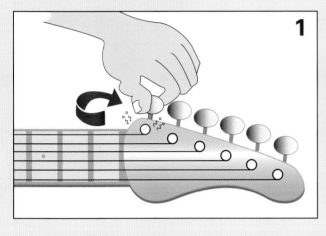

1 If the note is too high, or 'sharp', turn the machine head slowly clockwise to reduce string tension and lower the pitch. Keep the string ringing as you tune the note.

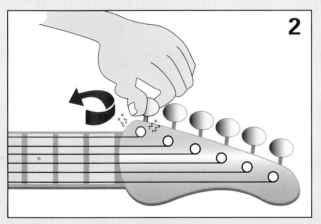

2 If the note is too low, or 'flat', turn the machine head slowly anti-clockwise to increase the tension on the string. This will make the pitch of that string higher.

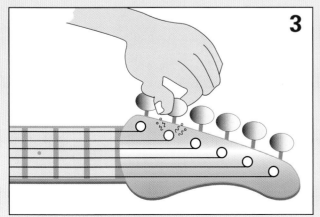

3 Tune the strings in order, from the 6th (controlled by the machine head closest to the neck) to the first. Carefully tune up to the note, listening to the string all the time.

Guitar Gear: Electronic tuners and pitch pipes

Using an electronic tuner is simple: you don't need to listen to the notes, since you tune the strings by eye. An electric guitar is plugged into the unit via a jack lead and the tuner monitors the pitch of each string, showing when it's tuned correctly. The unit also has a built-in microphone, so it can be used to tune the strings of an acoustic guitar too.

Pitch pipes are six pipes that each correspond in pitch to an open string on the guitar. Tuning from pipes relies on a good musical ear, and it can be difficult in a noisy environment, but pipes are a good way to 'train' your ears to tuning.

TABLATURE

Tablature is the most simple method of writing down guitar music. It's user-friendly, easy to understand and the main system of printed music used throughout this book.

Tablature, or TAB for short, is a method of writing music specifically for the guitar. It's shown on a 'stave' consisting of six parallel lines (as opposed to the five lines used in Standard Notation). It's quite simple: each horizontal line represents a string of the guitar, as shown opposite.

The top line (string 1) represents the thinnest, high-sounding string; the bottom line (string 6) represents the thickest, deep-sounding string.

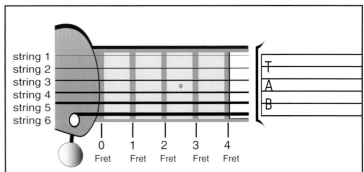

Fret positions

Instead of black and white note symbols on the lines, as you'd find in Standard Notation, TAB uses numbers that represent the fret you should put your finger behind (as opposed to on). The number is written on the line representing the string you should play, as shown below.

= Fret 1 on String 2

Fret numbering

The frets on a guitar are numbered from zero on the headstock rising up towards the body. Look at the diagram below: a string that's meant to be played 'open' (i.e. played without being fretted) is indicated by placing a '0' on that string. The first fret is depicted by a 1, the second by a 2, and so on.

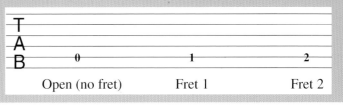

Open (no fret)   Fret 1   Fret 2

Basic Standard Notation Symbols

For the time being, the use of Standard Notation will be kept to a minimum. We have, however, printed some basic notation above the TAB, and this is represented by the symbols below. Each symbol stands for a measure of time between notes. The 'rest' symbols indicate periods of silence when you shouldn't be playing at all. When you see these symbols, count the relevant number of beats in your head before moving on to the next symbol.

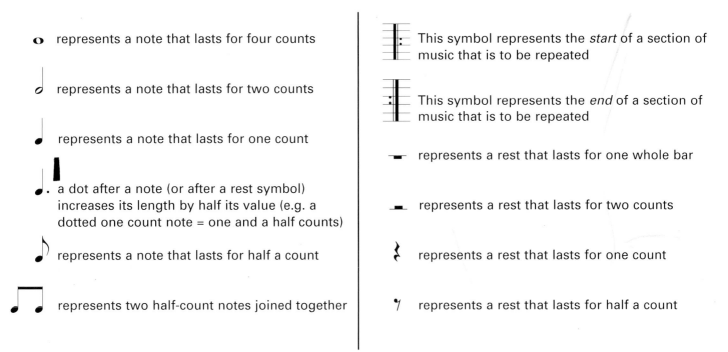

o   represents a note that lasts for four counts

♩   represents a note that lasts for two counts

♩   represents a note that lasts for one count

♩.   a dot after a note (or after a rest symbol) increases its length by half its value (e.g. a dotted one count note = one and a half counts)

♪   represents a note that lasts for half a count

♫   represents two half-count notes joined together

𝄆   This symbol represents the *start* of a section of music that is to be repeated

𝄇   This symbol represents the *end* of a section of music that is to be repeated

—   represents a rest that lasts for one whole bar

▬   represents a rest that lasts for two counts

𝄽   represents a rest that lasts for one count

𝄾   represents a rest that lasts for half a count

1. This marking highlights the bar to be played first time through a section that is to be repeated

2. This marking highlights the bar to be played second time through a section that is to be repeated

Other symbols

Other symbols, both in Standard Notation and in the TAB, will crop up. DON'T PANIC! We'll deal with them as and when you need to know what they mean.

Bars

Musical notes are grouped together in 'bars' of equal length. These are divided by vertical lines (see right). In this example, each bar groups together notes that make up the timing equivalent to a count of 1-2-3-4.

CHORD BOXES

Chords are the basis of good guitar playing. There are several ways of showing them, and one of the best is the simple chord box.

A chord is a series of notes that are played at the same time. Chords are at the root of all good guitar playing, and we'll be introducing new chords throughout the book. Chords can be depicted in various ways. We've chosen the chord box to illustrate them throughout, as it gives a clear visual representation of chord shapes.

Tablature on its side

Think of chord boxes as being like tablature turned on its side. The diagrams are simple graphic illustrations of the guitar neck: it's as if you're holding the fretboard of your guitar upright, with the frets and strings forming a kind of grid. The black dots show your left-hand finger positions. We'll also include photographs of hand positions to make them clear.

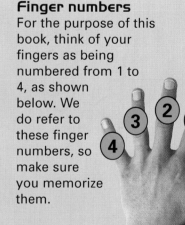

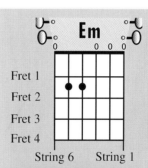

Finger numbers
For the purpose of this book, think of your fingers as being numbered from 1 to 4, as shown below. We do refer to these finger numbers, so make sure you memorize them.

Noughts and Crosses

All the symbols you'll see on a chord box are there to give you guidance.

A small '0' at the top of a chord box, above a string, means that you should play that string in the chord, but that it must be left 'open', with no left-hand finger pressing on it (i.e. 'unfretted').

A small 'x' above the string means that you shouldn't touch it at all when playing the chord.

The numbers below the box (see bottom right example) indicate the left-hand finger that's used to play each fretted note. It's important that you pay attention to these left-hand finger numbers, as using the correct fingers makes changing chords much easier.

Chord names

The letters at the top of the chord box (i.e. Em, Dm) indicate the name of the chord you are playing, e.g. Em = E minor, Dm = D minor, and so on.

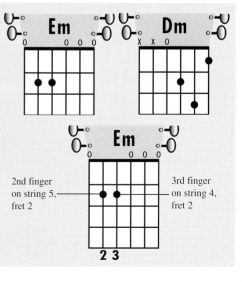

2nd finger on string 5, fret 2

3rd finger on string 4, fret 2

A GUIDE TO ELECTRICS

The electric guitar is one of the world's most popular instruments and many of today's greats began their careers playing a copy of one of the classic makes. This is your guide to the best and the rest.

Electric guitars haven't changed dramatically since the first designs were patented and the instruments mass-produced during the 1940s. The hardware, including bridges, machine heads and pick-ups (see page 6-7) have, however, become more sophisticated. This is a round-up of the classic electric guitar brands: their strengths, quirks, estimated price ranges and successors.

THE GIBSONS

Gibson is one of the most sought after guitar brands in the world. Renowned for quality of craftsmanship, the company pioneered Humbucker pick-ups, which give a rich, sustained sound. Allied to the Epiphone Company, Gibson began production in the 'Forties.

THE GIBSON LES PAUL

The Les Paul guitar was built for reliability, ease of use and richness of tone. It has a heavy body, a stop tailpiece, an accurate 'tun-o-matic' bridge, plus two Humbucker pick-ups, which contribute to the guitar's generous natural sustain (the length of time a note continues to ring after it is played).

The guitar's tonal qualities, combined with thick wire frets, make the Les Paul a dream to play, producing a jazzy, round tone at low volume, and a rich, sustained lead sound when played loud.

Price guide: £575 – £3275 approx. (new)
Favoured by: Jimmy Page (Led Zeppelin), Slash (Guns'n'Roses) and Steve Cradock (Ocean Colour Scene)

GIBSON SG

A close cousin of the Les Paul, the Gibson SG is famous for its shape. It has distinctive double cutaways that look like devils' horns. Some models have just one lead pick-up. The SG is favoured by blues and rock players for its raw, raunchy sound.

Price guide: £500 – £1100 approx. (new)
Favoured by: Angus Young (AC/DC)

Other famous Gibsons are notable for their eye-catching body shapes; for example, the Explorer, which has a peculiar rhomboid shape, and the Flying V, which has a body the same shape as its name.

THINLINE SEMI-ACOUSTICS

Brands: *Epiphone/Gibson/Guild/ Gretsch/Yamaha/Ibanez*

Thinline semi-acoustics are based on the early amplified jazz guitars. They are hollow-bodied, producing a rounded, warm tone, and have twin Humbuckers and simple controls. They sometimes feature a split bridge with a 'Bigsby' tailpiece – a design that has a crude spring tremolo, as played by Bernard Butler (ex-Suede).

The original and most copied model is the Gibson ES335, which is expensive, much coveted and played by Nick McCabe (The Verve) and Paul Banks (Shed Seven). Noel Gallagher and Paul Weller both play an Epiphone equivalent, and many other good versions are made by the companies listed above.

Clockwise from left: Steve Cradock (Ocean Colour Scene); a Gibson Les Paul Standard; a Gibson SG; Bernard Butler; the Blues Hawk Semi-Acoustic.

THE FENDERS

The first Fenders went on sale in the early 1950s. They were invented by Leo Fender, who tried to produce playable, lightweight guitars. Fenders are typified by single-coil pick-ups and a bright, ringing sound. The original Fender designs are virtually unchanged.

FENDER STRATOCASTER

The 'Strat' is the most famous of the Fenders. Few modern objects can claim to have retained the same design for more than 40 years, but the first Stratocaster went on sale in 1954. Its three single coil pick-ups and three- or five-way pick-up selector switch give a range of tones and sounds. The synchronized tremolo was made famous by Hank Marvin of The Shadows.

The guitar has a distinctive curved headstock and a contoured body for playing comfort. Twin cutaway horns enable easy access to the high frets. The sound produced by the Stratocaster has a bright, ringing quality. Popularized by Buddy Holly, it was later adopted by Jimi Hendrix, who created a wild range of sounds.

Price guide: £500 – £1000 approx. (new)
Favoured by: Eric Clapton, Jeff Beck (The Yardbirds), Ritchie Blackmore (Deep Purple), Mark Knopfler (Dire Straits) and Jimi Hendrix

FENDER TELECASTER

A chunky, workmanlike guitar, the Telecaster is great for chords and percussive playing because of its relatively short sustain and punchy sound. Originally intended to be a bargain guitar – hence its simple design – the Telecaster is now regarded as a classic.

Price guide: £400 – £600 approx. (new)
Favoured by: Keith Richards, Graham Coxon, Chrissie Hynde (Pretenders), Bruce Springsteen and Dave Gilmour (Pink Floyd)

Right: Pink Floyd's Dave Gilmour on his Telecaster.

Far left: Fender Stratocaster; Centre top: Fender Jaguar; Left: Placebo's Brian Molko and his growling Jaguar.

FENDER JAGUAR/ JAZZMASTER

Both the Jaguar and the Jazzmaster are sought after for their distinctive looks. Their two or three coil pick-ups have 1960s style on/off switches. They are favoured by Sonic Youth and Placebo, among others, for the bridge, which has a length of string behind the saddles that rings in a purposely out-of-tune way when struck.

Price guide: £500 – £800 approx. (new)
Favoured by: Sonic Youth, Placebo and Nirvana

OTHER MAKES
Yamaha SG2000

Similar to the Gibson in terms of playability and quality, with a distinctive shape. Not considered very trendy nowadays, but an excellent guitar nonetheless. Made famous by 1980s Scottish rockers Big Country.

MODERN ALTERNATIVES

Brands: *Washburn/Ibanez/Jackson/Charvel/Schecter*
All of the companies listed above have become respected guitar brands. As well as models based on the classics we've already mentioned, they have been free to build their own models, fitted with state-of-the-art electronics and hardware.

Pointed headstocks, two or more loud and abrasive Humbucker pick-ups, sophisticated 'locking' tremolos and internal power sources – such as batteries – all go to make the modern rock guitar a thing of the present.

Right: A Les Paul Special.

A GUIDE TO ACOUSTICS

The acoustic guitar has evolved over many centuries, and although it has been eclipsed in the glamour stakes by its electric cousin, it is still very much an instrument to be reckoned with.

The six-string, steel string acoustic guitar may be the hardest on your fingers, but it is almost certainly the favoured option when it comes to versatile acoustic playing. Nylon strings – which are found on most classical guitars – are less cruel, but if you want to play rock music, it has to be steel.

Although they all seem quite similar, steel-strung acoustics can vary enormously in quality and price. Cheap guitars are made from laminates – plywood to you and me – while expensive instruments are built using solid wood, valued for its tonal properties. Often, manufacturers combine both.

Some classic acoustic models to look out for are:

MARTIN

The modern acoustic guitar shape is generally based on the Martin Dreadnoughts of the 1920s and '30s. These guitars were designed for finger picking and strumming, and so had good string spacing, tone and projection. They often feature very decorative inlay work.

JUMBOS

Big bodied, booming acoustic guitars. They were designed for loud strumming and favoured by Elvis Presley, among others.

ELECTRO-ACOUSTICS

Electro-acoustics are acoustic guitars that have in-built pick-ups and, in some cases, pre-amplification. The most famous of these was made by Ovation

'The King of Rock', Elvis Presley, favoured the booming tones of a Jumbo acoustic.

in the 1970s. Ovation broke from tradition by making a guitar body from curved fibreglass and building in an electro-transducer pick-up that converted the string vibrations into sound, as opposed to a microphone-type pick-up.

The idea was to provide an amplifiable acoustic for the country and rock stars who were playing larger and larger venues, since amplifying a normal acoustic with a microphone could cause wild, uncontrollable and unwanted feedback.

The Ovations, as a result, had a tone all of their own: very bright, chiming but not quite as close to the sound of an acoustic guitar as some musicians would have liked. These days, every company produces acoustics with built-in pick-ups of varying quality.

YAMAHA

This consistent Japanese manufacturer makes excellent sturdy and clear-voiced acoustic guitars to suit all purposes – from expensive models for the discerning connoisseur, to straightforward, and very good, beginners' guitars. Prices start at around £100.

Left: The Vintage EYSO Acoustic.

Right: An Ovation electro-acoustic.

WHICH GUITAR?

If you're about to buy your first guitar, or you're thinking of changing from an acoustic to an electric, consult our practical guide.

If you haven't bought a guitar before, or you're about to buy your first electric, it's useful to have some information on possible pitfalls and what to look out for.

No reputable music shop would purposely sell you a defective instrument, but there are things you should be thinking about and checks you should be making all the same. For example, does the size of the guitar make it comfortable for you to play? Will the playing action strain your fingers? Are you confident that the guitar will stay in tune? And, more of a personal judgement, does the guitar make the kind of noise that you're after?

Whether you want to buy an electric or an acoustic guitar, you'll find that there's a vast selection to choose from. Stylistic points aside, there are also fundamental differences in sound and ease of playing.

SHOP AROUND

When it comes to electrics the choice need not be bewildering. As a rule, go for a sensibly weighted guitar with reasonable features, and shop around for the best price for the same model.

The bulk of electric guitars on the market are versions of the few basic models featured in this book. Copies and remakes of classic guitars can be very good value for money and shouldn't be thought of as inferior. A few 'phone calls to stockists will highlight any overpricing, and most music shops will be quite willing to give you a quote for a particular model.

One of the biggest-selling guitars is a Fender Stratocaster re-make by Squier. Original Fenders tend to cost a lot of money, which isn't always justified as the re-makes can often be as good as the originals. Expect to pay for authenticity and brand names. A vintage Stratocaster will sell for astronomical prices, but the commonly available Fender Squier series are also very good guitars, despite being copies. Alternatively, for around the same price you could go for a Yamaha Pacifica, which is a generally better and more consistent instrument than the Squier.

DON'T FOLLOW FASHION

Avoiding guitars that are in vogue will often save you money. Sales tags on Fender Jaguars went through the roof after Kurt Cobain was seen around the world wrenching his *Teen Spirit* from one. A more obscure make of twin Humbucker-type guitar won't be very hip and could therefore be a real bargain, so don't feel at all disappointed if you end up with a guitar that isn't a famous make and model – you might make that model of guitar famous! Guitars come in and out of fashion like everything else; if it feels good, plays well and sounds great, that's all that matters.

Left: the Jimi Hendrix Stratocaster; centre: the late Kurt Cobain thrashing his Strat; right: an ES175 Reissue.

Only £150

GUITAR BUYER'S CHECKLIST

The various knobs, switches and components on the modern guitar can baffle the novice buyer. Dispel confusion with these practical guidelines.

You are in your local music shop, facing a dazzling array of shiny new guitars. Now comes the business of deciding which features you want your own guitar to have. If you're still not sure what each guitar component does, base your mental checklist on the following points.

Guitar neck

Guitar necks feature different contours and depths. Find one that sits comfortably in your hand. If you have small hands, you might consider buying a guitar with a shorter scale, (i.e. less distance between the 1st and 12th frets), so that finger stretches in chords are a little easier for you. Telecasters – favoured by The Artist Formerly Known As Prince – tend to have a smaller scale.

Fretwire

Fretwire can come in different gauges: the thicker and wider it is, the more sustain you'll get – it's all down to personal preference. Play a few guitars with different gauge frets and see which you like.

Bridges

Bridges (see page 7) come in many shapes and sizes. They may be Fender-types – one or two pieces with adjustable saddles – or Gibson-types, with a split bridge. Both may feature a tremolo unit.
The quality and accuracy of the bridge has a direct effect on the sound of an electric guitar.

Above: A Fender-type bridge with adjustable saddles.

Tremolos

Tremolos come in two varieties: 'locking' tremolos have a clamp at the headstock, designed to keep your strings in tune no matter what you do to them. This necessitates fine tuners (small horizontal tuning machines) on the bridge. This ornate precision machinery can be a little fiddly for a beginner. The alternative is the cruder 'Strat'-type tremolo. Again, it depends on what you think you'll use your guitar for.

We'd advise against starting out with a guitar that has an elaborate tremolo, as you won't, at this stage, need to alter the pitch of your strings too often. Then again, all tremolo units can be fixed into a static position so that you can forget about them initially. Your music shop should be able to help you out.

Switches/Controls

A guitar can come with any number of switches: simple on-off switches; three-way selectors (shown here); five-way selectors; coil-tap, to switch between single coil and Humbucking sounds (see below); and rotary controls. Keep it simple at first; everything on a guitar can be customized later.

Pick-up types

Pick-ups are either single coil (right), giving a bright, treble tone, or Humbuckers – two magnetic coils that give a louder, rounder response, with more sustain. Humbuckers are favoured by the rock and blues fraternities. Modern guitars sometimes have a coil tap fitted, which lets you

switch from single coil to Humbucker without having to change your pick-up.

A standard double-coil Humbucker.

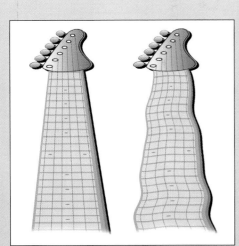

Neck

The neck of the guitar should be straight, without warps or bends. To check this, look down the neck from the top nut to the bottom. You should be able to see that the neck and fretboard form nice parallel lines going into the distance. Now swivel the guitar through 90 degrees and check from both sides. Look for any kind of bowing. If you're keen on the guitar but there's some minor bowing, the truss rod – a steel pole that runs through the centre of the neck – can be adjusted to compensate. Ask the shop to set it up for you before you purchase the guitar.

Fretboard

Look out for grooves worn in the frets under the strings. A little wear is fine and to be expected on a second-hand guitar, but any great ruts and trenches could cause you real problems when you're playing.

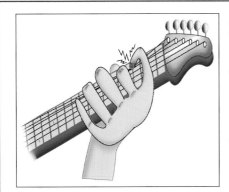

Action

The playing 'action' describes the distance between the guitar's strings and the fretboard. This shouldn't be excessively high or too low, and should remain reasonably consistent as it goes up the neck. Too high will tire your hands and hurt your fingers; too low and the strings will buzz. The action can be adjusted if necessary, so ask your supplier.

Electrics

Make sure you have listened to a second-hand electric guitar through an amplifier before you buy it. Check that all the switches work without cutting out (i.e. going quiet); make sure that each pick-up works; ensure that the output socket works; listen for any buzzing or crackling noises, or sudden loss of volume.

Acoustics

Check for any cracking on the body. Make sure there are no weak spots on the surface of the guitar due to broken internal struts. Check this by pressing gently on the front of the guitar.

Weight/Balance

A guitar should feel balanced and comfortable to play. Check this by playing it while standing up.

Buying Tips

● When trying out an electric guitar, remember it will only sound as good as the amplifier it's playing through. If you already own an amp, ask the music shop to let you play the guitar through a similar one; if you don't have an amp, you'll have to buy one sooner or later.

● Unscrupulous shops have been known to sell poor-quality electric guitars by demonstrating them through state-of-the-art effects units into a top-quality amp. Beware: the guitar will sound different when you play it through your home stereo. Heartbreak is inevitable, so it's unwise to listen to a guitar through an effects unit in the shop.

Left-handed Players

It used to be the case that a left-handed player had to buy a right-handed guitar, turn it upside-down and re-string it the opposite way. Although there are now left-handed versions of most guitars, many left-handed players prefer to play a right-handed guitar as this allows their naturally stronger left hand to be used for the more intensive and intricate fretwork.

Hendrix: left-handed genius.

TYPES OF STRING

The type of string you fit on your guitar not only affects the instrument's sound, but also its playability and the wear and tear on your fingers. This guide will help you choose the right ones.

Guitar strings are measured by their 'gauge', or thickness. There are broad categories of string gauge, designed to give optimum intonation – something we'll discuss in greater detail later.

The most common gauges for a set of electric guitar strings are 0.009 in for the 1st string, up to 0.042 in for the 6th string. String 1 gauges as low as 0.007 in are only really suitable for very fast, high fret solo playing, since these lighter strings make 'bending' and other advanced techniques much easier.

Steel and bronze strings

Strings for electric guitars are made from fine grade steel. The top three strings are each made of one single strand, while, on the lower three strings, a strand acts as a core, around which a very fine grade of steel wire is machine wound.

(Some jazz players who prefer a heavier gauge also opt for a 'wound' 3rd string).

Acoustic string gauges tend to be a little heavier: a medium gauge set of acoustic strings will have a 1st string of around 0.012 to 0.014 in, and a 6th string measuring around 0.052 to 0.056 in. Unlike most electric sets, the 3rd string is usually 'wound'.

It can happen to anyone: '70s idol Marc Bolan playing with broken strings during a live performance.

Acoustic guitar strings have a steel core, like electric guitar strings, but the winding on the heavier strings around the core tends to be bronze or phosphor-bronze, rather than steel. This is because acoustic guitar strings are designed to make a 'real' sound, and so use the better tonal qualities of bronze, whereas electric strings are designed to produce maximum effect for the pick-ups – a property of steel.

Anchoring the strings

Strings for both steel-strung acoustics and electric guitars have a steel or brass ball at one end. This is used to anchor the string to the bridge. Check carefully when buying: some electric guitar string sets have 'piano-wound' endings. Avoid them at this stage, as they are intended for use on bridges that have been specially set up.

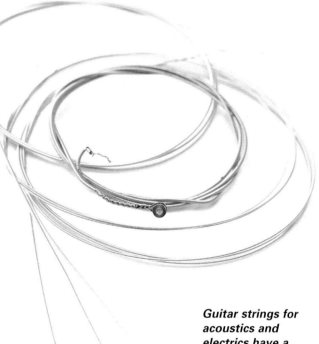

Guitar strings for acoustics and electrics have a metal ball at one end to anchor the strings to the bridge.

Nylon core

Classical guitars use different types of strings altogether. Originally, the top strings were made of cat gut, but nylon is now universally used. It is an easier, more consistent material to work with – and it's more politically correct than using animal products too. A fine metal thread is wrapped around a nylon, fibre or silk core on the lower strings.

Fitting steel strings on a Classical guitar can cause irreparable damage to the guitar, as these delicate instruments are not designed to withstand the far greater stresses imposed by tougher strings.

REPLACING DAMAGED STRINGS

Strings may need to be changed for a number of reasons – too worn, too dirty, poor tuning or bad playing technique. Here's how to deal with it.

Your guitar strings are the most important part of the instrument – take them away and what are you left with? Follow our step-by-step guide over the next few pages to learn the correct method of replacing strings and caring for your equipment.

When to change

How often you should change your guitar strings is largely a matter of discretion or necessity. Some recording artists like to have a new set on their guitar at each session for the bright, ringing, metallic tone that new strings always have. Others prefer the sound of old, well-worn strings, free of trebly overtones.

If you can see that the winding – the fine outer layer of wire wrapped around the lower strings – is broken at any point, you'd be advised to change the string as soon as you can, as it's about to snap. Keeping strings clean makes a marked difference to how they feel on your fingers and also extends their life considerably.

The basic kit for changing strings: a lint-free cloth, pliers and – useful, but not really essential – a machine head-winder. The following pages explain step-by-step how to change strings.

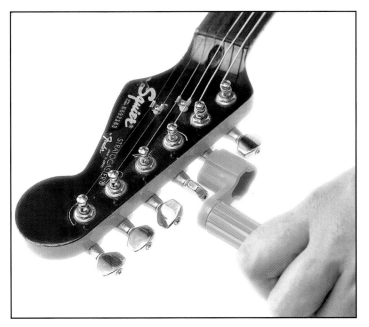

Above: Although it's not essential, a machine head-winder takes the strain out of fitting and tuning strings. Working like a simple gear, it helps to achieve a smooth and even winding around the tuning post when fitting a new string, and makes it quick and easy to slacken an old one.

Causes of breakage

If your strings seem to be breaking regularly, it could be down to a number of reasons, e.g.,
- tuning the string too high – never tune 'above' the note you're tuning to;
- bad right-hand action – hitting the string too hard;
- poor plectrum technique;
- incorrectly set up bridge.

We'll deal with the last point on pages 62-63. In the meantime, medium strings and a nylon plectrum should prevent too much breakage. Heavy, stiff plectrums may be favoured by heavy-metal players for fast soloing but, when combined with light strings, breakage is inevitable.

The ability to replace strings quickly while on stage is a skill honed to a fine art by some roadies. Wilko Johnson, guitarist with '70s R&B combo Dr Feelgood, had a roadie who was so good at changing strings that if Wilko broke a string mid-solo on his Fender Telecaster, a new string was in place and in tune by the time Wilko got to the end of the solo – never having missed a single note!

CHANGING ELECTRIC STRINGS

Changing, or replacing, strings isn't difficult when you know how, but a string that isn't put on correctly can cause all sorts of problems.

Like most practical tasks, changing your electric guitar's strings is quite straightforward if you follow a few basic steps. Some people just slap them on and hope for the best, but they get a nasty shock when they ping off, or fail to tune. Follow our foolproof guide.

STEP 1
If the string isn't broken, but is old or difficult to tune, first slacken it off as much as possible by turning the tuning head until the string is loose.

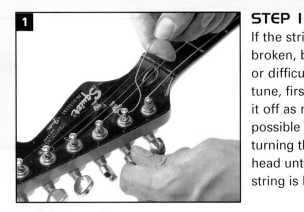

STEP 2
Carefully remove the string from the tuning post. If it's difficult, a small pair of pliers will make the job much easier.

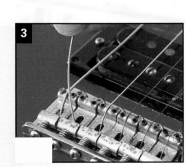

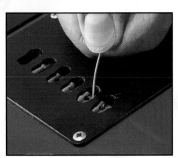

STEP 3
Thread the string back through the bridge. Depending on the style of bridge, you may have to thread the string back out through the body of the guitar (as on a Stratocaster-type) or just out of the back of the bridge (as on a Les Paul-type). Some sophisticated tremolo units have quite tricky access through the back of the guitar – take your time and be patient.

STEP 4
Now that the string is off, wipe the area it covered on the neck with a dry cloth, to clean off any dirt that's accumulated. If the string isn't broken, don't throw it away; it might be useful later. Coil it up and put it in the packet that your new string came in.

STEP 5
Take the end of the new string that *doesn't* have the ball on it and thread it back up through the bridge until it appears over the saddle. Pull the string through until it can't come any further.

STEP 6
Thread the other end of the string through the tuning post. Make sure that you've got the correct post – it's an easy mistake to make!
Now, leaving some slack in the string (enough that you can pull it 10 cm or more away from the neck), make a tight loop around the post in the *opposite* direction to the one in which the string will be tightened (see **Figure 1** on the next page), so that you're beginning to wind it. Wind *anti-clockwise* for the bottom (thickest) three strings and *clockwise* for the top (thinnest) three strings. If your tuning machines are all on one side, as they are on Fender-type guitars, they should all be turned *anti-clockwise*.

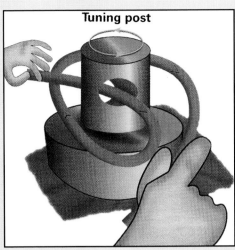

Tuning post

FIGURE 1
Thread the new string through the tuning post, winding the slack string around it in the opposite *direction to the one in which the tuning post tightens. If the tuning machines are on the left-hand side of the headstock, wind the string* clockwise *around the post; if they're on the right-hand side of the headstock, wind the string* anti-clockwise.

STEP 7

Start tightening the string. Once it starts to tighten up and isn't flopping around any more, you should have wound it tautly around the post three or four times. More is acceptable, but any fewer and the string could slip.

STEP 8

When you've securely wound the new string, you'll probably have some extra length dangling from the posts. You can leave this if it doesn't bother you, but it's a good idea to cut it off, as it can get in the way of your left hand, or worse, poke you in the eye during some serious riffing practice!

To get rid of excess string, first bend it into a little kink, close to the post; then, using a pair of wirecutters or pliers, snip the extra length off. Kinking the string ensures that its outer layer doesn't unwind.

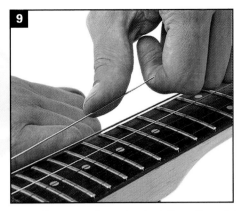

STEP 9

Tune the string using your usual method.

New strings have a lot of 'give' in them, so to save having to constantly re-tune, you can take the stretch out of new strings by holding the string close to the 12th fret and pulling it gently up and away from the neck. You should feel it 'give' a little. Once it's secure you'll need to re-tune it.

STEP 10

A change in the tension of one string will have an effect on the others, so if you change one string, you'll have to re-tune all six strings again. Also, changing just one or two strings could well result in a difference of tone between the brighter, new strings and the older, more worn ones. Therefore, it is often better to change all six strings for the sake of consistency.

Expect new strings to stray a little out of tune at first. They'll soon settle down.

You can purchase guitar strings individually or in packets of six. Electric guitar players often find that they regularly break the same string – usually the thinnest one.

CHANGING ACOUSTIC STRINGS

The instructions for changing acoustic strings work along the same lines as those for electrics, but there are a few crucial differences.

STEP 1
If the string isn't broken, but is old or difficult to tune, first slacken it off as much as possible by turning the tuning head until the string is loose.

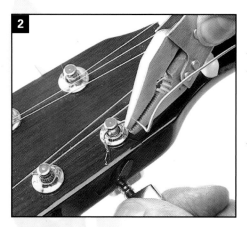

STEP 2
Carefully remove the string from the tuning post. If it's difficult, a small pair of pliers will make the job much easier.

STEP 3
Acoustic strings are often held in the bridge by small bridge pins, which are easily broken if you don't take care.

To loosen them a little, press the string down towards the body of the guitar. This should loosen the pin enough for you to pull it out with your fingers. If this doesn't loosen it sufficiently, either grip the head of the pin with pliers and gently ease it upwards, or try inserting a coin in between the pin and the bridge and levering it up gently. If it still won't budge, try to insert your hand into the guitar's soundhole and push the pin out from the inside.

STEP 4
Now that the string is off, wipe the area it covered on the neck with a dry, lint-free cloth, to clean off any dirt that's accumulated. If the string isn't broken, don't throw it away; it might be useful later. Coil it up and put it in the packet that your new string came in.

STEP 5
Slide the ball end of the new string into the bridge using the bridge pin. Push the pin down until it's in as far as it can go.

STEP 6
Thread the other end of the string through the tuning post. Make sure that you've got the correct post – it's an easy mistake to make!

Now, leaving some slack in the string (enough that you can pull it 10 cm or more away from the neck), make a tight loop around the post in the *opposite* direction to the one in which the string will be tightened (see **Figure 2** on the next page), so that you're beginning to wind it. Wind *anti-clockwise* for the bottom (thickest) three strings and *clockwise* for the top (thinnest) three strings.

STEP 7

Start tightening the string. Once it starts to tighten up and isn't flopping around any more, it should be wound around the post three or four times, until it's taut. Try to avoid overlapping the windings of the string as this will result in tuning inconsistencies.

STEP 8

There will now be some extra string flopping around from the posts. You can leave it if it doesn't bother you, but it's a good idea to cut it off, as it can interfere with your left hand action. To do this, first bend the string into a little kink close to the post, then, using a pair of wirecutters or pliers, snip the extra length of string off. This ensures that the outer layer of the string doesn't unwind.

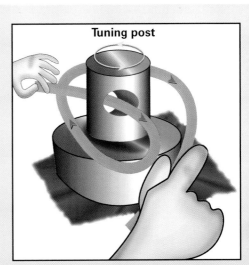

Tuning post

FIGURE 2
Thread the new string through the tuning post, winding the slack string around it in the opposite direction to the one in which the tuning post tightens. If the tuning machines are on the left-hand side of the headstock, wind the string clockwise around the post; if they're on the right-hand side of the headstock, wind the string anti-clockwise.

STEP 9

Tune the string as usual.

New strings have a lot of 'give' in them, so to save having to constantly re-tune, you can take the stretch out of them by holding the string close to the 12th fret and pulling it gently up and away from the neck. You should feel it 'give' a little. Now re-tune it.

STEP 10

A change in the tension of one string will have an effect on all the others, so if you change one string, you'll have to re-tune all six strings again.

CHANGING NYLON STRINGS
Classical/Spanish/Flamenco guitars

If you're playing on a nylon strung guitar, changing strings is relatively easy. Thread one end through the bridge from the soundhole side until about 8 cm comes through, then loop it back round and under itself. Now wind the remainder back around the string and tie it off to form a tight hold – try to copy the neighbouring strings' attachment. Pass the other end through the hole in the horizontal tuning post, and then keep turning the machine head until you have enough wound around the post for the string to keep its tension, and start tuning.

AMPLIFYING AN ELECTRIC

If you want to play electric guitar, you'll need to buy an amplifier. Here's a guide to choosing the best one to suit your needs.

Left:The Fender Twin, a classic valve Combo.

No electric guitar is complete without the means to amplify its sound. When choosing an amplifier, you need to decide how much volume you want and how portable you need the set-up to be. You should, in addition, consider the different tonal properties of the various amps available.

Naturally, your choice of amp also depends on what you can afford and prices can range from a moderate £60 to a hefty £1,500 for a single unit. There are two basic types of amplifier: the *combo*, so-called because it is literally a combination of amplifier and speaker, or a separate *head* (amplifier) and *cab* (speaker cabinet).

Left: Marshall have been producing valve-powered amps for more than 35 years.

(home hi-fi systems are often quoted as having an output of 100s of watts) it's because a guitar amplifier's output is measured in 'watts RMS', which refers to an average sustained output level, unlike the wattage readings for hi-fis, which only represent potential, or peak, volumes.

For practice, recording and home use, an amp with 30, 40 or 60 watts output is plenty. When playing on stage or with a full band, however, you might find that you need the power of a larger combo, or head and cab, although the walls of amplifiers that many rock stars use are as much a sign of vanity as a need for volume. By contrast, for instance, Radiohead's Jonny Greenwood achieved the great chord sound on *Creep* by playing through a Fender Champ, a small combo of about 30 watts at most.

Rick Parfitt of Status Quo against a 'wall' of Marshalls.

Heads and Cabs
Heads tend to be heavy, as they contain the amplifying electronics. They usually have a far more powerful output than combos. The speakers that the heads are teamed up with must be able to cope with the amp's output, so check before buying. Cabs invariably contain more than two speakers, often in multiples of four, and their considerable weight necessitates carrying handles on each side.

Combos
Combos combine an amplifier with one or more speakers in a relatively portable box, usually with a carrying handle on the top. They range from tiny practice amps to stage-worthy, hefty monsters.

What Wattage?
The level of an amplifier's output volume is measured in 'watts'. Small combos are usually rated from 30 watts upwards, while heads and cabs tend to begin at a minimum of 100 watts. If you think this sounds low

Walls of sound
The Marshall Head and Cab became a pre-requisite feature of a band's 'backline' (on-stage equipment). Some rock bands soon tried to out-do one another for the sheer numbers of cabinets they could cram on stage, creating a wall of speakers designed to make them look as 'heavy' as they sounded (see Rick Parfitt pic above).

Valve values
Another important distinction is between *valve* (or *tube*) amps and *transistor* (*trannie*) amps. Once, all amplifiers used vacuum-filled glass valves in the amplification stage. These produce a rich tone and the sound qualities they exhibit while 'overdriven' (amplified to their limit) are now highly sought after. The main drawback of valves is their frailty; they break easily and the element inside the valve can eventually deteriorate. A solution to this problem came in the form of transistor, or 'solid state' amplification.

Lightweight transistors

Transistors are durable and, like hi-fi amps, produce volume without distortion. Transistors require fewer heavy electronics to power them and, as a result, trannie amps are generally much lighter than their valve counterparts.

Valve & trannie combos

Transistor amps were all the rage until guitarists realized that old valve amps, with all their problems and tonal idiosyncrasies, actually sounded better: they are 'warmer' in tone and more responsive. Many modern combos combine valve and transistor technology to achieve the best of both worlds, using sophisticated transistor circuitry for the pre-amplification stage and warm-sounding valve volume for post-amplification.

Above: A mini Fender Twin practice amp.

Buying an amplifier

Amps come in numerous shapes and sizes, but a portable, compact combo is perhaps the only real option for home use. It is sensible to try lifting the amp on your own before you buy. Looks can be deceiving and even a small amp may prove weighty.

There's a good range and quality of inexpensive amps available. You can buy tiny amps for practice or busking, such as the little Pignose amp, which has a volume knob in the shape of a pig's snout. (You can buy a 10 watt Pignose for around £100.) Both Marshall and Fender also make miniature replicas of their bigger classics, so you can have a famous name without breaking the bank. Fender even make a tiny Twin (pictured above), which is only about 4 inches high.

Equally, you don't need hundreds of features on your amp if you are a first-time buyer. Second-hand amps can be real bargains. However, make sure the amp is thoroughly checked over before you buy it, especially in the case of a valve amp.

Vintage valve amps are now seen as desirable and modern manufacturers copy the design features of old amps – tweed covers and large knobs – even if they don't copy the outdated electronics.

Amplifiers for acoustics

The great advantage of an acoustic guitar is that you don't need an amplifier unless you regularly play at big venues. However, if you prefer the power of an electric on your acoustic, you can buy excellent amps designed especially to suit. You'll need to have either an in-built pick-up in the guitar, or have one permanently or temporarily fitted. Amps for acoustics are designed to clearly reproduce the instrument's sound.

Above: Oasis favour the distinctive retro looks of Orange's valve heads and cabs.

Pete Towshend of The Who 'road-tests' another cabinet for Marshall.

THE AMPLIFIER'S CONTROLS

How to use the various controls you'll find on the average amp.

As an electric guitar player, you're bound to use an amplifier at some point. At first glance, amps can appear more complicated than they really are. Different manufacturers have different names for the same functions but, broadly speaking, all amps have a similar range of controls. Although you won't necessarily find all of these controls on one amp, this guide highlights most of the features you'll come across.

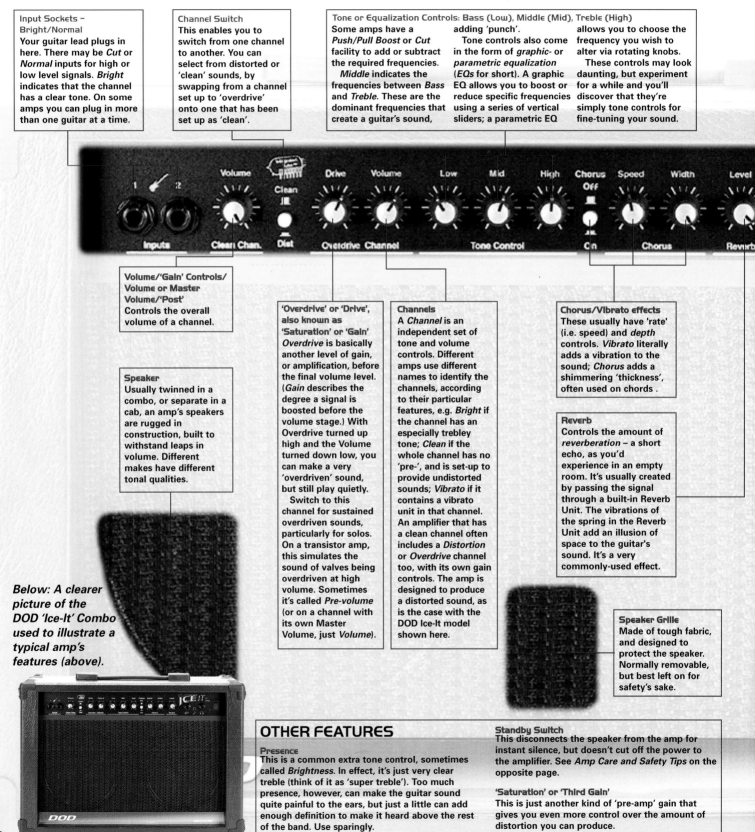

Input Sockets –
Bright/Normal
Your guitar lead plugs in here. There may be *Cut* or *Normal* inputs for high or low level signals. *Bright* indicates that the channel has a clear tone. On some amps you can plug in more than one guitar at a time.

Channel Switch
This enables you to switch from one channel to another. You can select from distorted or 'clean' sounds, by swapping from a channel set up to 'overdrive' onto one that has been set up as 'clean'.

Tone or Equalization Controls: Bass (Low), Middle (Mid), Treble (High)
Some amps have a *Push/Pull Boost* or *Cut* facility to add or subtract the required frequencies.
    Middle indicates the frequencies between *Bass* and *Treble*. These are the dominant frequencies that create a guitar's sound, adding 'punch'.
    Tone controls also come in the form of *graphic-* or *parametric equalization* (*EQs* for short). A graphic EQ allows you to boost or reduce specific frequencies using a series of vertical sliders; a parametric EQ allows you to choose the frequency you wish to alter via rotating knobs.
    These controls may look daunting, but experiment for a while and you'll discover that they're simply tone controls for fine-tuning your sound.

Volume/'Gain' Controls/
Volume or Master
Volume/'Post'
Controls the overall volume of a channel.

Speaker
Usually twinned in a combo, or separate in a cab, an amp's speakers are rugged in construction, built to withstand leaps in volume. Different makes have different tonal qualities.

Below: A clearer picture of the DOD 'Ice-It' Combo used to illustrate a typical amp's features (above).

'Overdrive' or 'Drive',
also known as
'Saturation' or 'Gain'
Overdrive is basically another level of gain, or amplification, before the final volume level. (*Gain* describes the degree a signal is boosted before the volume stage.) With Overdrive turned up high and the Volume turned down low, you can make a very 'overdriven' sound, but still play quietly.
    Switch to this channel for sustained overdriven sounds, particularly for solos. On a transistor amp, this simulates the sound of valves being overdriven at high volume. Sometimes it's called *Pre-volume* (or on a channel with its own Master Volume, just *Volume*).

Channels
A *Channel* is an independent set of tone and volume controls. Different amps use different names to identify the channels, according to their particular features, e.g. *Bright* if the channel has an especially trebley tone; *Clean* if the whole channel has no 'pre-', and is set-up to provide undistorted sounds; *Vibrato* if it contains a vibrato unit in that channel. An amplifier that has a clean channel often includes a *Distortion* or *Overdrive* channel too, with its own gain controls. The amp is designed to produce a distorted sound, as is the case with the DOD Ice-It model shown here.

Chorus/Vibrato effects
These usually have 'rate' (i.e. speed) and *depth* controls. Vibrato literally adds a vibration to the sound; *Chorus* adds a shimmering 'thickness', often used on chords .

Reverb
Controls the amount of *reverberation* – a short echo, as you'd experience in an empty room. It's usually created by passing the signal through a built-in Reverb Unit. The vibrations of the spring in the Reverb Unit add an illusion of space to the guitar's sound. It's a very commonly-used effect.

Speaker Grille
Made of tough fabric, and designed to protect the speaker. Normally removable, but best left on for safety's sake.

OTHER FEATURES

Presence
This is a common extra tone control, sometimes called *Brightness*. In effect, it's just very clear treble (think of it as 'super treble'). Too much presence, however, can make the guitar sound quite painful to the ears, but just a little can add enough definition to make it heard above the rest of the band. Use sparingly.

Standby Switch
This disconnects the speaker from the amp for instant silence, but doesn't cut off the power to the amplifier. See *Amp Care and Safety Tips* on the opposite page.

'Saturation' or 'Third Gain'
This is just another kind of 'pre-amp' gain that gives you even more control over the amount of distortion you can produce.

AMP BACK PANEL FEATURES

Pre-amp Out Socket
Allows you to plug your amp into a more powerful amplifier to increase its volume capacity.

Ext. Speaker Socket
Allows an external speaker to be powered by your amp.

Line Out Socket (Unbalanced/Balanced)
Sends a signal from your amp to a mixing desk, e.g. so that it can be used for recording live sound.

Effects Loop Socket
Allows you to plug an effects unit into the amp.

Headphone Socket
Very useful for practising quietly at home. A good feature to look for when buying your first amp.

On/Off Switch
This normally appears on the front panel, but can sometimes be found tucked away at the back on old '60s amps.

Foot Switch Socket
If the amp has switchable channels, built-in effects or Reverb, you'll invariably have a foot switch with a jack plug that plugs in here. This lets you change any function you wish without having to stop playing.

Neil Young and Crazy Horse playing 'live', in front of a stage set of enormous, fake Fender 'Bassman' amplifiers.

Guitar Gear:
Amp Care & Safety Tips

Amps can be delicate and even potentially dangerous. Look after them and yourself!

• Never tamper with the internal electrics of your amp when the power is switched on.

• Check the earthing on your plug. A broken or badly fitted plug is dangerous.

• Keep liquids away from amps. The old rockers' habit of leaving a pint of beer on an amp has caused plenty of amp – if not human – casualties.

• If you're moving an amp around, make sure it's secure. Combos tend to be top-heavy and valves are almost as delicate as lightbulbs – so no sudden shocks. Some players protect their amps with 'flightcases', sturdy metal boxes with internal padding, on wheels; but even an inexpensive vinyl amp cover will save on wear and tear.

• When switching an amp on or off, turning the Master Volume *down* prevents blowing a fuse, damage to the speakers and sending your neighbours into a state of shock. If it has a 'Standby' switch, use this if you're turning the amp off for short periods, or before you switch it off altogether. Valves burn out if constantly heated and cooled down. The Standby switch was invented to prevent this from happening.

27

AMPLIFYING ACOUSTICS

Acoustic guitars can be fitted with a special pick-up to amplify their 'natural' sound.

An acoustic guitar may need to be amplified in order to hear it above the sound of drums, keyboards, or other instruments in a band. However, it's difficult to amplify the instrument using a microphone and a public address (PA) system because the soundbox is likely to resonate with the amplified version of its own sound. This would, in turn, be re-amplified, resulting in booming, uncontrollable feedback. The solid body and pick-ups of the electric guitar were largely designed to eliminate this problem.

Tackling feedback problems

A makeshift way to amplify an acoustic guitar is to stuff a piece of fabric or screwed-up newspaper into the soundbox, then point a microphone at it. This method aims to prevent any amplified sound from leaking back into the guitar's body and it stops a feedback 'loop' occurring. Unfortunately, it also means that you lose much of the instrument's natural sound, as the strings can no longer resonate in the soundbox.

The development of 'transducer' pick-ups, pioneered by the Ovation company in the 1970s, all but eradicated the problem, allowing feedback-free amplification through PAs for the first time. These pick-ups work by detecting string vibrations through changes in pressure, rather than acting like microphones and amplifying air vibrations.

Adopted by stadium rockers and country artists around the world, the modern 'electro-acoustic' guitar (see page 14) – used by guitarists as diverse as Noel Gallagher and Garth Brooks – began life with the development of the transducer pick-up.

Singer and guitarist Simon Breed using a slot-in Seymour-Duncan soundhole pick-up in his Fender acoustic.

Heavenly Record's artiste Beth Orton, amplifying her acoustic by using a clip-on, saddle-mounted pickup.

Acoustic pick-ups

Nowadays, there is a variety of pick-ups available, from saddle transducers to models that already have the lead attached, and which can easily be slipped into a guitar's soundhole without the need for any alteration to the instrument.

Such dedicated pick-ups often combine transducer and conventional pick-up technology and give a remarkably 'true' acoustic sound.

Reliable brands:
• *Seymour Duncan, Tanglewood* and *Dean Markley*.
Price guide: £70 – £150.

A dedicated amp

Acoustics with pick-ups are often 'direct injected' (DI'd) into a PA – even small 'acoustic' venues tend to do this. It does, however, leave the sound and tonal quality of the guitar in the hands of the 'front of house' sound engineer. A dedicated amp allows the guitarist to control the sound of his or her own instrument.

Using an electric guitar amp, with its high levels of gain, poses more feedback problems and the harmonic distortion of a 'warm' valve amp isn't normally desired by acoustic players. However, the sophistication of modern pick-ups for acoustics means that you can use an electric guitar amp, provided that you go easy on the volume.

Amplification designed specifically for acoustic guitars has recently come into its own. Biased towards tone controls, these amps feature sophisticated EQs to fine-tune the sound, and have clean channels and speakers custom-built to faithfully reproduce the tones of an acoustic instrument.

Reliable brands:
• *Fender, Laney, Yamaha* and *Acoustic*.
Price guide: £200 – £800.

NAMING NOTES

As well as learning to tune your strings by ear, it's useful to know the names of the notes you are playing, plus their equivalent fretted notes.

Every time you practise, it is important to keep your guitar tuned to sound the correct notes. It's also helpful to know the names of the notes that you're tuning up to, and which fretted notes sound the same as the open strings.

For this exercise, tune the guitar as normal, then try checking these notes out for yourself, using the following procedure: Fret string 6 at fret 5. Now play the open 5th string. If the guitar is in tune, the fretted and open strings should sound the same note (A). Moving up from the lowest to the highest strings, you'll find that the 5th fret note of each string sounds the same as the note of the next open string up. The 2nd string is the exception; it sounds the same as the note on the 4th fret of the 3rd string (B).

These notes are set out in a diagram below, which represents your fretboard, with the lowest string (E) at the bottom of the diagram, like a line of TAB.

Open string notes and their fretted equivalents

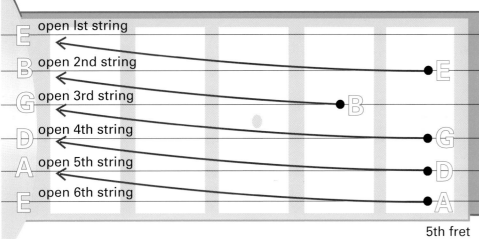

5th fret

- *The 2nd string at the 5th fret is the same note as the open 1st string -* **E**.

- *The 3rd string at the 4th fret is the same note as the open 2nd string -* **B**.

- *The 4th string at the 5th fret is the same note as the open 3rd string -* **G**.

- *The 5th string at the 5th fret is the same note as the open 4th string -* **D**.

- *The 6th string at the 5th fret is the same note as the open 5th string -* **A**.

All notes up to fret 5

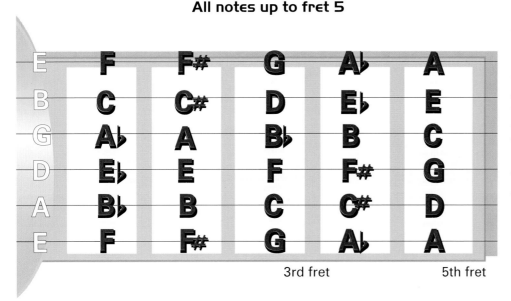

3rd fret   5th fret

Note recap
The diagram on the left shows the notes given above, plus the names of all the notes in between, up to the 5th fret. It works like this:

- String 6 played open is the note E. When fretted behind fret 1, it makes the note F. Hence, on the diagram, there's an F behind the 1st fret on the 6th string.

- ♭ represents a note called a 'flat'

- ♯ represents a note called a 'sharp'

Flats and Sharps
Flats and sharps are an essential part of musical theory that will be covered in greater detail later.

CHOOSING AND USING LEADS

Leads are an essential, but often overlooked, part of an electric guitar player's kit. A failing lead can ruin a performance, so it's worth knowing how they work, what they do, and which to use.

Although leads may seem to be largely the domain of electric guitarists, an acoustic guitar player using a pick-up will also need to know what's what when it comes to leads.

Varieties

Most guitar leads are mono, 'jack-to-jack' leads. One end is plugged into the guitar and the other end into an amplifier. They should not be confused with speaker leads, which are designed to connect the amp to the speaker cabinet. Speaker leads are built to carry high levels of power over short distances, rather than transport the subtle and minute changes in an instrument's signal. If used to connect your guitar to your amp, they are not going to give you a good quality sound and they are very likely to pick up a lot of electrical interference.

Guitar leads carry a tiny alternating signal between your guitar and your amp. You might hear a buzz when you plug in your guitar, or when you hold one end of a lead that is already plugged in to your amp. This happens because touching both the tip and the outer cylinder of the jack-plug at the same time partially closes the electrical circuit.

Construction of leads

The cable of a mono lead has an inner wire core that runs to the tips of its jack-plugs at either end, and an outer wire core that is joined to the long

A close-up of a mono jack-plug, showing its construction.

cylinder of each jack-plug.

The join of the lead to the jack-plug can break under the stress of normal usage, making the signal break up and eventually cut out. Some leads have heavy-duty cabling and connections to prevent this, and offer longer reliability as a result. Buying cheaper leads may seem like making a saving, but the inevitability with which they will break makes this a false economy.

Quality

Cheaper quality leads can pick up interference from external sources and will not, therefore, carry the signal to your amp as clearly. In higher quality leads, the outer core is 'braided' or cross woven around itself. This provides greater protection against interference and reduces the chances of the wire breaking under stress.

A close-up of the outer braided core of a good quality lead.

Cheaper leads tend to have only straight outer wires.

Some leads are 'oxygen free'. This means that no air is allowed between the wire core and its rubber surround during construction, which again prevents interference and eliminates 'noise' such as crackling and rustling through your amp when the lead is moved. Cables with only a thin PVC surround will make a lot more of this unwanted noise.

Price guide: from £5 – £20 approx.
Brands: *Whirlwind/Dimarzio/Orange*

Lengths

The length of lead you should buy depends on your needs. One or two metre lengths are adequate for home playing, but may prove restrictive on stage. Conversely, very long leads are only necessary for playing on big stages – you'll need the length when you're running along the gantries at Wembley Stadium! Very short connector leads, or double-connector jacks, are ideal for linking effects pedals or units to each other.

Short connector, or 'patch', leads and double-connector jacks.

Curly or straight?

If a coiled lead is pulled to its full extent, the player can feel a gradual increase in tension, making it less likely to get yanked out of its socket than a straight lead. The great disadvantage of coiled leads is their awkwardness – a coiled lead will not slip smoothly under your strap, and as a result fewer and fewer players use them.

Types of jacks

There are a few varieties of standard quarter-inch jack-plugs (so-called because the plug is the 'male' Jack to the socket's 'female' Jill). Some have two-piece connectors with an unscrewable sleeve, which allows you to check the soldering join between cable and jack, and repair it if necessary; others are made of moulded vinyl. The latter cannot be repaired if the connection breaks. Jacks-plugs often have a protective spring at their base to cushion movement and take any strain.

A right-angled jack-plug.

Right-angled jacks are useful for plugging into effects units or into amps, when you need the jack and the lead to take up as little space as possible. However, they are awkward if used in an indented socket, such as the socket on a Fender Strat.

Stereo leads

Although most guitars have a mono output, you might come across guitars with stereo sockets. These are useful if you are working with stereo effects units, in a recording studio, or if you want to create a 'wall of sound', by sending each of the two mono signals that make up a stereo signal to separate amplifiers.

Below: A quarter-inch stereo jack-plug (l) and a stereo 'cannon' jack (r).

Although stereo guitars were briefly in vogue in the 'Eighties, they were in fact pioneered on some eccentric models in the 'Sixties.

Stereo guitars require stereo leads. These can have either normal quarter-inch sized jacks that have two lines on the jack, or 'cannon' jacks, like the leads used for a microphone. Cannon jacks have a three-pin socket arrangement at one end of the lead, while the other end can either feature a quarter-inch jack or another cannon jack.

Coloured leads

Brightly coloured or dayglo leads may seem garish, but their great advantage is that they remain visible under stage lighting. A visual aid that makes for quick and easy set-ups is to use colour-coded leads; for example, red to the guitar, yellow to an effects pedal, and so forth.

Guitar Gear: Wireless Sets

The practical, but expensive, alternative to leads.

Wireless set-ups are popular with acts that move around a lot or play very large stages, because they bypass the physical problems of very long leads by leaving nothing to trip over or get tangled up in. Based on the same technology as wireless vocal microphones, they feature a transmitter unit, usually clipped onto the player's belt or pocket, into which the guitar is plugged. This sends a signal on a specific radio frequency to a receiver unit that is plugged into an amp. However, they're expensive in comparison to leads, and if more than one unit is used, care must be taken to keep their frequencies separate.

PJ Harvey using a wireless unit, with the transmitter pack clearly attached to her waistband.

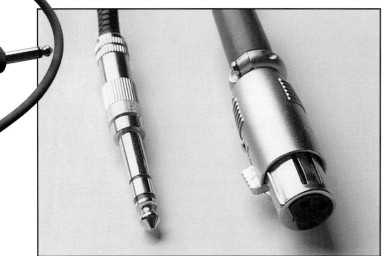

POSSIBLE SET-UPS

There are many different ways of connecting up your guitar – here are two sensible arrangements, one acoustic, one electric.

As a general guide to how you should employ different leads to best effect, here are two potential set-ups for electric and acoustic players. In the electric set-up, a long, straight lead runs from the guitar to an effects pedal (the longest lead of the set-up), allowing maximum movement. The pedal is joined to two effects units which are linked via a short connector lead. The signal is relayed back to the amp by another long lead.

The acoustic has a similar set-up, the difference being that the last stage joins a tuner to the amp via another short lead.

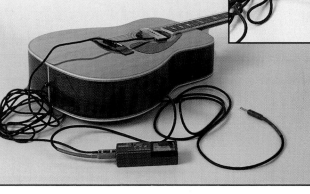

Right: An acoustic's pick-up lead, plugged into a tuner, with a long, straight lead running from the tuner to an amp or D.I. box.

Above: A possible set-up for an electric. From l to r: A long straight lead from the guitar to effects pedals; short patch leads between the pedals; a long lead to an amp.

Guitar Gear: Lead Safety & Care

Any professional guitar player will tell you that one of the most common performance problems is failing leads, heralded by a tell-tale crackling and sudden loss of volume. Here's how to prolong your leads' lives.

• To prolong the life of your leads, never put the connector jacks under any great strain. Avoid sudden yanks on them by passing the lead under and through your guitar strap before plugging it into the guitar's socket. This way, if you should accidentally tread on your lead, the strap – and not the lead – will take the strain. In addition, this will avoid putting any unwanted strain on your guitar's socket.

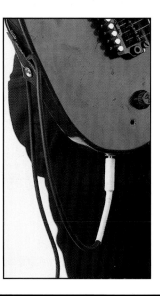

• Try not to stuff your leads haphazardly into your guitar case. Before putting them away, coil straight leads up evenly and carefully by loosely looping them in one hand. Gently twist the cable at the top of each loop to prevent kinks.

• Another way to avoid strain on the leads is to use 'gaffer' tape to secure them in place. This fabric-reinforced PVC tape is often used to secure leads to amps, leads to effects, effects to the floor, etc. It's easy to tear off from the roll but surprisingly strong. A roadies' cure-all, Sonic Youth's Thurston Moore has even used it as a makeshift bandage to hold together wounds on his hands, caused by over-vigorous strumming!

STRAP IT ON

Whether on stage, busking or just in your room, if you want to play standing up, you'll need a strap.

The scalloped body 'contours' of many solid-bodied guitars, such as Stratocasters and Les Pauls, are designed to fit against the curves of the player's body and are most comfortable in the standing 'performance' position. Acoustic players also need to play standing up sometimes; hence the need for a strap.

Strap styles

Straps can be made of leather, nylon or cloth, and come with varying degrees of decoration. An embroidered strap for an acoustic was once a ubiquitous part of 'Sixties gear. Guitar straps can be a part of the look of a guitarist's stage set. In the 'Eighties, Eric Clapton and Sting (amongst many others) sported Fender's own-brand straps. 'Metallers' like Lemmy from Motorhead have been known to use empty bullet cartridges for straps, while rockers such as Thin Lizzy went for studded leather every time, and Neil Young is rarely seen without a strap that is embroidered with doves and peace symbols.

A cheap remedy for strap fatalities – a rubber washer.

A good strap should be wide enough to spread the weight of a guitar across the shoulder. Back pain is a common ailment among guitarists, so avoid narrow straps that concentrate all the weight of a solid-bodied guitar in one place. The strap should be adjustable for height, either via a range of slots or notches at one end of the strap, or by a sliding buckle, so that the guitar can hang at the optimum level.

Strap adjusted for optimum guitar position, with the neck tilting slightly upwards.

When properly adjusted for height, the bottom of an electric guitar should sit on or around the hips, with the neck tilting slightly upwards, leaving the shortest distance for the fretting hand to cover. It is a matter of personal preference, so find a happy medium. Wearing the guitar in a 'low slung' position may look cool, but it limits your playing by placing greater demands on your arms and hands. At the other extreme, wearing the guitar very high on the chest can be equally limiting. With the correct position and the right strap, you should feel confident enough to let go of the guitar entirely, and it should stay in place. However, you might have to compensate for the uneven distribution of weight that some solid-bodied guitars have.

Keeping straps in place

Attach a strap to the buttons on the bottom and upper left of the guitar's body. Sometimes this second button is found on the heel of the neck. The wide rims of strap buttons are designed to hold the strap in place. However, a common accident that befalls guitarists is that the guitar slips off the strap and plummets towards the ground. Like every other area of guitar hardware, however, designs have improved over the years. You can now buy 'locking' or 'click-on' straps, making mishaps like this impossible. A good, cheap tip is to use a rubber washer, like those found on beer bottle stoppers. Once your strap is on the button, slip one of these over the button and you'll find that it's almost impossible for your strap to slip off.

Strapping on acoustics

If, as is often the case on acoustic guitars, there is only one strap button on the bottom of the body and nowhere else, tie the free end of the strap onto the guitar with a short length of strong cord – a shoelace is ideal – by passing it

A strap attached to the head of an acoustic with strong cord.

under the strings on the machine head side of the top nut, and tying it securely on the other side. Make sure that there is no spare cord hanging in the way of your left hand.

GUITAR CARE AND MAINTENANCE

How to keep your guitar gleaming and well maintained to make playing easy, prevent future problems and protect your investment.

Some guitar maintenance and repairs need expert attention, especially if the guitar in question is an expensive or vintage instrument. But there are a few things you can do that will prolong the life of your guitar and save you money on repairs. There's nothing like the feeling of playing a well-maintained guitar, with new strings and a smooth, clean fretboard. The reasons are not just cosmetic – keeping your guitar in good condition maintains the playability, as well as the value, of your guitar.

1. Keeping the body clean

Most guitar bodies can be wiped with just a clean cotton cloth that has been slightly dampened with warm water, and then 'buffed' with another dry cloth. Expensive French polish finishes on classical guitars (distinguished by their rich, deep-looking burnish) should only be cleaned in this manner.

2. Cleaning the strings

Every time you play, your fingers leave a little moisture, grease and sweat on the strings. The salt from the sweat causes rust, and the build-up of dirt will dull your guitar's tone and cause tuning problems.

Clean your strings carefully, one by one. Loosen each string off a little and slip a lint-free cloth under and around it just at the top nut. Then, gently slide the cloth along the string – you'll be surprised by the amount of dark, caked-on dirt that comes off! This works on all types of strings – steel, bronze and nylon.

Guitar polish, lubricant and lemon oil.

Which polish?

Guitars with synthetic or cellulose finishes need polish. Do not use normal household spray polishes. These tend to be silicone-based and the silicone will permeate the wood of the guitar, making any future finish work, such as a re-spray or a customized finish, very difficult. You should use only purpose-made guitar polishes, which can be bought in any good music shop for around £2.00 per bottle.

3. Cleaning the fretboard

Frets can be cleaned with a special fret cleaning polish, but care should be taken not to allow any of this metal polish onto the wood of the fretboard.

How you treat the wood of your fretboard depends on what it's made of and how it's been 'finished'. Some guitars have a lacquer finish on their fretboards, as is the case with the Fender Stratocasters that have a blond maple fretboard. This should be treated in the same manner as a delicate guitar body, i.e. wiped with a damp cloth and then buffed with a dry one. Most guitars have an 'unfinished' fretboard, usually made of rosewood or ebony, chosen for their dark, hard and smooth grain. These woods like to be 'fed' by being treated with oil every now and then. Lemon oil, which can be bought at good specialist guitar shops, should be applied with a cloth and left on for a few minutes. Remove the dirt that builds up on either side of the frets with a cloth wrapped around your thumbnail, or a plectrum, while the wood is soft from the oil. Then vigorously give the whole thing a polish with a dry cloth.

4. Gathering dust

Dust and fluff can often accumulate inside the body of an acoustic or the soundhole of a semi-acoustic. Either blow this out or use a vacuum cleaner – carefully!

A paintbrush is a handy tool for brushing out the little build-ups of fluff and dust that accumulate in those tricky, hard-to-reach places such as around bridge parts and under the strings above the top nut.

5. Maintaining humidity

The woods of both classical and steel-strung guitars need a consistent level of humidity (the degree of moisture in the air around them) to prevent any warping or loss of tone. Packets of silicate drying

agents are available. These can be left in the guitar or in its case, but they only prevent excessive dampness; there are now sophisticated pads that fit into an acoustic's soundhole which maintain a constant level of humidity.

ELECTRIC GUITAR MAINTENANCE

I. Metal work

The chrome-plated parts on an electric guitar, such as the bridge or the pick-ups, can be cleaned with a burnishing cream. Any gold-plated parts should just be wiped with a soft cloth. If you find any rust on your guitar, for example on the alloy bridge parts that constantly come into contact with sweaty hands, soak the rusty part in a little oil; standard '3 in 1' multi-purpose oil is ideal. Any excess oil should be wiped away before replacing.

2. Switches and sockets

If the pick-up selector switch on your electric guitar crackles slightly when it's switched into different positions, try spraying it with a little WD40 (a water and dust repellent spray for car spark plugs and other electrical contacts). However, this is only a short-term remedy and should not be used as a cure-all.

If you experience any problems with the socket, such as loss of volume and crackling, you need to take your guitar to a specialist repair shop, or be prepared to do some soldering. We will look at some basic soldering repairs to sockets on pages 70-71.

CLEAN AND TIDY

The best way of keeping your guitar in top-notch condition is to prevent the build-up of grease and grime in the first place. Get into the habit of wiping your guitar's body and its strings (thereby preventing any rusting) after every playing session, before putting it away in its case.

A GUIDE TO TUNERS

From the simple to the extraordinary, we look at some of the tuning devices available.

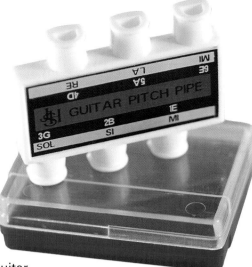

A set of JHS plastic pitch pipes and box.

There are a whole host of tuning devices on the market, which meet a wide range of needs. Although electronic tuners are now very common, and like all other electronics have become cheaper and more widely available in the last decade, due to developments in technology, the more traditional tuning devices can be just as useful. Apart from budget, the kind of device that you choose should be based on your requirements and the circumstances in which you have to tune your guitar. If you're going to be tuning while the rest of a band is playing, you'll need a unit you can plug directly into (to cut out all extraneous noise). Furthermore, if you'll be tuning in the semi-dark of stage lighting, you'll need a well lit visual display.

Tuning forks

Once the main tuning reference for musicians of every kind, a tuning fork has two prongs that vibrate when struck at the frequency of a note, usually named on the stem of the fork. Small enough to keep in your guitar case, they can't go out of tune and as a cheap accessory are always a useful standby. They are particularly useful for tuning an acoustic guitar, as touching the end of a tuning fork on the body of an acoustic produces a loud, resonating note. Since they make the player tune to one reference point, they also develop his or her sense of pitch. The more often that you tune your guitar, the easier you'll find it becomes, as you literally train your mind and ears to hear the right notes.
Price guide: £2 – 5 approx.
Makes include: *John Walker/Wittner*

Pitch pipes

These are a set of small pipes that you blow into to produce the correct note for each string, making a sound similar to a harmonica. Having a note for each string shortcuts the need for relative tuning

(see page 40), but they are actually quite difficult to tune to. Although they are cheap and easy to keep in a guitar case, years of use can affect their reliability and make them less accurate than you'd think.
Price guide: £4 approx.
Makes include: *Hohner/Ernie Ball/JHS*

Electronic tuners

Electronic tuners range from straightforward hand-held devices and foot pedals to sophisticated 'rack' systems. Thanks to microchip technology, over the years these have become cheaper and smaller, to the extent that some affordable models are now good enough to be 'industry standard'.

Basic models

Basic electronic tuners can only recognize the open string notes individually, usually via a built-in microphone, and so the notes need to be selected one by one on the tuner. Despite this drawback, they are still an adequate and useful tuning tool, and some do include both manual and automatic note selection.

A SEIKO multi-functional tuner.

Price guide: £15 – 30 approx.
Makes include: *Frontline/Arion/Korg*

Chromatic tuners

These offer a variety of displays and inputs. The more advanced

Danelectro's 'Fifties-styled foot pedal tuner.

electronic tuners can be switched to a 'chromatic' function, so-called because a 'chromatic scale' includes all the notes found at every fret on any particular string – in piano terms, all the black and white keys.

Whereas the cruder microchips of basic electronic tuners can only detect one specified note at a time, chromatic tuners can detect and name any note. In fact, they will name and display (usually via LED lights or a VU meter's 'needle' indicator) the name of the nearest note and how flat or sharp you are in relation to it. An extended 'upper range' sensitivity also allows you to check the tuning of notes at the higher frets, which is useful for checking intonation (the consistency of tuning all the way up the neck). The better the quality of the tuner, the greater the degree of accuracy. Most tuners are accurate to +/– 3 cents, which is three hundredths of a semitone (remember, one fret equals one semitone), but the best are accurate to +/– 1 cent or even higher.

Price guide: £70 – 150 approx.
Makes include: *Boss/Aiwa/Seiko/Hohner/Korg/Yamaha*

Guitar-mounted tuners

Some tuners are literally mounted onto the body of your guitar, either with a clamp or a sucker. They detect string vibrations through the guitar's body via a pressure-sensitive 'piezo' pick-up. Their only real drawback is that some players might find the addition of a large, limpet-like tuner to their guitar a little unattractive.

Price guide: £15 – 60 approx.
Makes include: *Matrix/Onboard Research Corporation*

Rack or stage tuners

Some highly sophisticated versions of electronic tuners are designed to be incorporated into a guitarist's 'rack' (which might contain an amplifier, a pre-amp, EQ's and a host of other effects units, all permanently wired 'in-line'). Racks provide a visual guide to the tuning of every note played (usually via LED lights or VU-type meters). However, they are relatively expensive and are of little use unless you need to use a rack system.

Price guide: £150 – 300 approx.
Makes include: *Korg/Yamaha/Boss*

The KORG DTR1 – a deluxe rack, or stage, tuner.

Strobe tuners

Very unusual but a lot of fun, these futuristic machines have a stroboscopic display; the tuning lights 'strobe' out of phase until the desired note is in tune, when they appear as a continuous light. This technology was first developed to tune the engines of US military aircraft! These are only likely to be found in very sophisticated guitar workshops or studios.

Price guide: £600 approx.
Makes include: *Peterson*

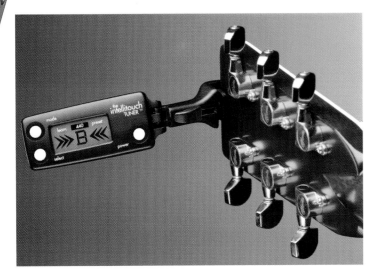

Left: The Intellitouch Tuner works by detecting vibrations in the guitar's body.

A TUNER'S CONTROLS

An in-depth guide to some of the features you'll find on an electronic tuner.

An electronic tuner has become a standard feature in a guitarist's set-up. Although the actual specifications and the names given to each function may vary from model to model, they tend to have broadly the same facilities. This model, a Boss TU-12, is an industry standard – the tuner equivalent of a Fender Strat. As such, other makes and models of tuners will share some, if not all, of its features.

PITCH

A key feature of the more sophisticated tuners is pitch control. Sometimes, you might be playing along with an instrument that cannot be tuned, such as a piano or a harmonica. The instrument might sound in tune with itself but not with the tuner, because it has a slightly higher or lower pitch. A chromatic tuner will show you how much flatter or sharper this instrument is. For example, the note A – at fret 2 on string 3 – is a wave that vibrates at 440 Herz (double vibrations per second). If the instrument you are tuning to has its A at 442 Herz, all you have to do is select 442 as the pitch of note A on the tuner's pitch control and all the other notes will be adjusted accordingly, allowing you to tune up as normal. When you've finished using the tuner that has been re-set to this new pitch, your guitar should be perfectly in tune with the erring instrument.

LED NOTE INDICATORS

In 'Guitar' mode, these lights refer to the markings from 6E to 1E below, showing which string has been selected (by pressing the Down and Up buttons). The needle indicator will show how close the string is to the right note.

When the tuner is in 'Chromatic' mode, the LED lights refer to the row of letters above, showing the nearest note to the one being played, while the needle again shows how near to this note the played note is. The extra light to the right, marked by a '#' symbol, shows up if the note isn't one of the seven letter notes but a note in-between. For the purpose of this tuner, they're called 'sharps'. The note at fret 2 of string 6, for example, is an F sharp, so both the F light and the # light will be lit.

LED LIGHTS

The left-hand LED light illuminates when the note you are playing is lower than the desired note, the right-hand one lights up when it's above. Both light up if the note is in tune.

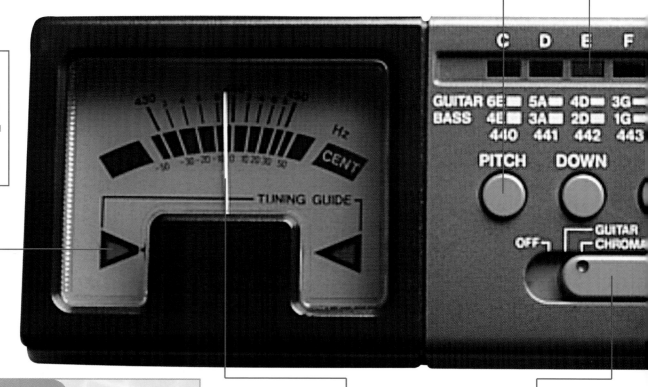

VISUAL DISPLAYS

On a tuner, a Visual Display Unit will show you how flat (below the desired note) or how sharp (above the desired note) your chosen guitar string or note is, and also which note it is.

Visual displays can consist of several kinds of lights, including LEDs (light emitting diodes), LCDs (liquid crystal displays) or stroboscopic lights in sequence (as on the new BOSS-T2). They may have a VU needle, which will move either side of a zero point, indicating how sharp or flat the played note is. The speed, accuracy and readability of an electronic tuner's visual display are crucial. You should be able to see if you are in tune at a glance. Some displays look fine in daylight, but can prove illegible under stage lighting or in a dark rehearsal room. Others are back-lit, designed to be visible at all times, while many displays have luminous markings.

NEEDLE METER

In 'Guitar' or 'Chromatic' mode, the needle shows variation from a central zero position (which would indicate that the note is in tune) in cents (percentage of a semi-tone). When in 'Pitch' mode, it indicates a reading on the Herz scale above.

FUNCTION SELECTOR SWITCH

Allows you to choose between 'Chromatic' or 'Guitar' (string-by-string) mode.

Elliot Smith, acclaimed for his delicate vocals and plaintive acoustic playing, carefully tuning up in-between songs.

Guitar Gear:
Getting the best from
your tuner

Every tuner has its own idiosyncrasies. Here are some tips for easy operation.

• An electronic tuner works best if it is given one clear note at a time. When you play just one string, others vibrate in sympathy with it, creating overtones that the tuner will detect and try to measure. To minimize these 'sympathetic' vibrations, try to damp all the other strings with the palm of your right hand. Play the string with your fingers rather than the plectrum, as plectrums can create 'false notes', or overtones. If you are tuning an electric, turn up the volume and tone controls.

A Rapco A/B box.

• Using a tuner 'in-line' (i.e. patched in as a constant component of an amplified set-up) allows you to check tuning without having to change any equipment around. An amp's effects loop output or headphone socket provides a convenient out signal for in-line tuning. Alternatively, connect your tuner in sequence like an effects pedal, but plug it in the sequence before any effects pedals.

An extra 'pro' option for an on-stage tuning set-up is an A/B box. This is a simple channelling device that routes the guitar signal to one of two outputs – A or B. Having an amp connected to route A and a tuner to route B allows a player to switch to the tuner alone while tuning up, thus sparing the audience the unpleasant sound of a guitar being tuned mid-performance.

• Electronic digital chromatic tuners use a lot of power compared to other effects units, so turn them off after use and replace the batteries regularly, as failing power will lead to inaccurate readings. Some makes have an LED that flashes when the battery needs replacing. Better still, use an AC converter power supply.

An AC converter power supply unit.

INPUTS

Input Socket

Electronic tuners use an input socket into which you send your guitar's signal via a jack lead, and/or a built-in microphone. The latter works best with an acoustic or semi-acoustic guitar, as the unamplified sound of a solid-bodied electric might not be picked up over any background noise. The ability to plug in also means that an electric guitarist need not wait for the rest of his band to be quiet while he tunes up.

Through Facility

Many tuners have a 'through' facility with an input and output socket. This allows the guitar signal to pass through a tuner to an amp without it being affected. The great advantage of this is that with a chromatic tuner set up in-line, the player can see whether any note being played is in tune, eradicating the need to stop playing when tuning up.

RELATIVE TUNING
You'll often find yourself without a reference note to tune to, so here's how to perform relative tuning – an invaluable skill.

A tuner will tell you whether or not you're in tune, but you still have to do the work of tuning your guitar. We suggest that you tune to some kind of reference point. However, you will inevitably find yourself without a reference, which is when you need to use relative tuning. This technique uses information from the 'Naming Notes' feature on page 29, which covers the names of the open strings and their fretted equivalents.

Relative tuning helps to train your 'musical ear', i.e. your ability to recognize notes and hear when they are in tune with one another. It is called 'relative' because you end up with all the strings in tune relative to each other, but not necessarily to anything else.

One string needs to be used as a reference note; in this case the bottom E, the open 6th string. (You could just as well use string 1 (E) as the reference and follow this relative tuning procedure in reverse.) If you're unsure of the pitch of the string, it's best to err on the low side and have slightly loose strings rather than strings tuned so high that they might break.

sound the same.

STEP 1
Play the 6th string at fret 5, the note A, to which string 5 should be tuned. While the note is still ringing, play open string 5. Now adjust its tuning and play both again until they sound the same.

STEP 2
Once string 5 is in tune with string 6, use the same procedure for string 4. Play string 5 at fret 5 and the open string 4 together, then tune string 4 until it sounds the same.

STEP 3
String 3 is tuned in exactly the same way as strings 4 and 5. Play string 4 at fret 5 and then play string 3 open, and tune string 3 until it matches the fret 5 note.

STEP 4
Tuning string 2 is a little different from the others. This time, play string 3 at fret 4 and then tune open string 2, until they make the same note.

Finger tip

KEEPING BOTH STRINGS RINGING
Tuning is easier if you can hear both the string you are tuning and the fretted note you are tuning to at the same time. To this end, try this useful trick: play both notes, then reach over with your right hand and tune the open string note while both strings are still ringing. You should hear the two notes come together.

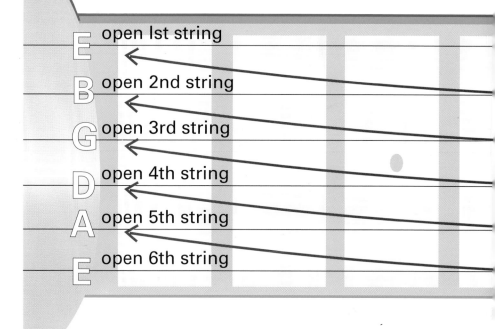

open 1st string E

open 2nd string B

open 3rd string G

open 4th string D

open 5th string A

open 6th string E

REFERENCE TUNING

If you do have some kind of reference source handy, here's how to tune to it. You can use any note as a reference note, played from a tuning fork, pitch pipe or any other instrument.

Let's say you have a tuning fork that makes an A note. Using the 'Naming Notes' guide on page 29, find the string or fret that has the same note name – in this case, the open A string (string 5).

Tune the string to the tuning fork, letting them ring together so that you can clearly hear how close they're getting. Next, tune all the strings above it, using the relative tuning method. Finally, play the 6th string at fret 5 and compare it with the open 5th string.

Tuning to a keyboard

If you have a keyboard or piano handy, this diagram shows the keys to which the open strings of a guitar should be tuned. You can either tune them string by string, or tune one to the correct keyboard note and then tune the remaining strings using the relative tuning method.

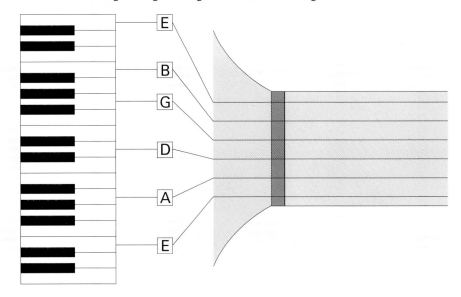

STEP 5

To tune the first string, apply the method used for strings 3, 4 and 5 once again. Play the 2nd string at fret 5 and then the open string 1, and tune it until it's identical.

STEP 6

Now pluck strings 6 and 1 together. They should sound like the same note, but two 'octaves' apart. (see below). You can also check some fretted notes against each other to see how well you've tuned your guitar. For example, string 5 at fret 7 should sound the same as the open string 6 note; in this case, both notes sound an E, but one octave apart. Similarly, string 4 at fret 7 should sound the same as the open string 5, which is an A, but one octave up. For matching other fretted notes, refer to the diagram on page 29.

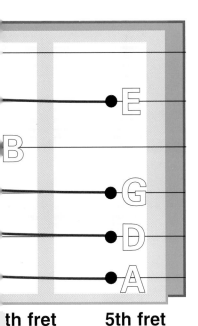

th fret   5th fret

- *Tune string 1 to the same note as fret 5 on string 2 – the note **E**.*

- *Tune string 2 to the same note as fret 4 on string 3 – the note **B**.*

- *Tune string 3 to the same note as fret 5 on string 4 – the note **G**.*

- *Tune string 4 to the same note as fret 5 on string 5 – the note **D**.*

- *Tune string 5 to the same note as fret 5 on string 6 – the note **A**.*

- *Take string 6 – the note **E** – as your reference, or starting point.*

WHAT IS AN OCTAVE?

Most guitars have a range of three octaves (apart from electric guitars with 24 frets, which have a range of four octaves). The note at fret 12 of each string, marked by a double dot, is an octave up from the open string note. So why an octave, or 'eighth' note? This is because, in a major scale (as in the traditional Do, Re, Mi, Fa, So, La, Ti, Do), the note that you reach at the end of the scale has the same name as the one you started out with, and it's the eighth note in the sequence.

PEDAL TO THE METAL

A look at the pedals used by famous guitarists: Fuzz, Volume and Distortion, plus the distinctive Wah-Wah.

Over the years, effects units have seen similar changes in fads and fashions as other areas of guitar gear. The first effects units were forms of Distortion, Fuzz, Reverb and Delay units. During the last couple of years, state-of-the-art multi-effects processors have become hugely popular, most notably Zoom multi-effects units. However, in keeping with the fashion for all things retro, the original crude versions of pedals are enjoying a comeback – their fat, friendly tonality is a relief from the crystalline clarity of digital effects.

Effects are not the sole domain of electric players. Acoustic guitarists often use Chorus, Reverb, Delay, Flange and even Distortion. Getting a grounding in what each effect does will prepare you for any future studio or stage work, where all of the effects described in this guide will feature heavily. In terms of price, most foot pedals range between £30 and £120.

Use of an effect can define the sound of a guitarist or band; The Pretenders are forever associated with Chorus as much as Hendrix is with Wah-Wah. Some players use them discreetly, just to add a little excitement to a song, whereas others – such as My Bloody Valentine's Kevin Shields, Robin Guthrie from the Cocteau Twins and Stereolab's Tim Gane – have made an art form out of creating unearthly, exhilarating sounds through layer upon layer of effects, producing a sound that's barely recognizable as a guitar.

immediacy of the 'dirty' Chicago blues sound. Dave Davies of The Kinks found that sawing into the cone of his amp's speaker produced a pleasing, rasping 'fuzzy' sound, which was great for solos and riffs. The sound was copied by the Fuzz box – a basic electronic circuit designed to give a fuzzy sound. Fuzz boxes feature a combination of a basic volume control with a tonal filter.

A classic example of a 'fuzzed' riff is the Stones' *Satisfaction*, while a more recent example is *A Girl Like You* by Edwyn Collins. Bass players also use Fuzz boxes – check out the bass line to another 'Sixties classic, Sly and the Family Stone's *Dance To The Music*.

Used by: Jimi Hendrix, The Rolling Stones and many others
Classic models: *Electro-Harmonix Muff Fuzz/Colorsound Fuzztone*

ProCo's RAT distortion pedal – a reliable and powerful 'stomp box'.

Distortion

Distortion gives a harder edged noise than Fuzz and is great for power chords and solos. At the press of a pedal, a Distortion unit can mimic the sound of an amplifier driven to full volume, while leaving individual notes with a much clearer definition than the buzz of Fuzz.

Distortion units have similar circuitry to Fuzz boxes. They work by exaggerating specific frequencies of a guitarist's sound and their different pedals give tonal qualities that range from a hard-edged metallic attack to a smoother bluesy sound. When stomped on, a good Distortion box will give a slight leap in volume and power from the guitar's clean sound; part of the fun of Distortion units is in the stomp, followed by an immediate rush of volume and power. This is demonstrated to full effect by Graham Coxon on Blur's *Song 2*, and in the heavy tracks on Nirvana's

Fuzz

In the late 'Fifties and early 'Sixties, guitarists looked for earthy sounds to emulate the

JD-2 Fuzz Face – a retro sounding Fuzz box with a kooky but rugged design.

Foot pedals
Early effects units had manual switches that were inconvenient to flip on and off. It soon became apparent that the easiest way to use effects was to have a pedal (or 'stomp box') at the guitarist's feet.

Foot-switch units
Larger units, such as the Roland Space Chorus or Watkins Copycat, can be mounted on top of a player's amp, and turned on and off with a basic foot switch.

Multi-effects units
Thanks to microchip technology, many units now feature a wide variety of individual effects – these can be used separately or in any combination with each other.

Rack units
Sophisticated rack units are used both in studios and in stage racks. They are usually digital units that have widely adjustable parameters as well as the typical pre-sets.

Digital vs analogue
All effects started out as analogue technology (transistors or tape) but now have digital equivalents. Just as with valve vs transistor amps, both have their own qualities. On the whole, analogue units tend to create more unwanted noise, while digital ones will give you a 'cleaner' sound.

Volume

A Volume pedal is usually a large foot pedal that acts exactly like the volume control on an electric guitar. When fully depressed, the pedal increases the signal to its full source volume; when rocked back, the volume decreases. You can achieve some good guitar tricks by using a Volume pedal, such as swelling the volume of a chord after it has been strummed, or softening the attack of solo notes – easing them up to produce an effect not unlike a violin. This sort of thing was originally done by adjusting the volume control with your right hand, but using a foot pedal instead makes it easier to concentrate on your playing. As soon as Volume pedals hit the UK, they were snatched up by John Lennon and Keith Richards, who both made clever use of them on their *Help!* and *Between The Buttons* albums, respectively.

Adding some oomph – a GD Volume pedal.

Used by: Johnny Marr (*Meat Is Murder*) John Squire (*Second Coming*), Nick McCabe (*A Storm In Heaven*) and Mark Knopfler (*Brothers In Arms*)
Classic models: *Ernie Ball/Jim Dunlop/Schaller*

Nevermind. Digital Distortion units create distorted overtones on very specific frequencies, exploited to the full by Steve Albini, whose guitar sound with Big Black owed a lot to the Digitech Distortion pedal.
Used by: Nirvana, Oasis, Blur, Supergrass, Radiohead and many others
Classic models: *Boss DS-1(a.k.a. Roland EF1)/DS-2/ ProCo RAT/Electro-Harmonix Big Muff*

Overdrive

Overdrive grew out of heavy rock acts needing greater sustain and Blues players wanting the sound of 'vintage' valve amps at full whack. It gives a cleaner sound than Distortion or Fuzz, and is good for solos that require very long sustained notes and for hammer-ons and pull-offs.

Rocktek Overdrive pedal – an economy unit that does the job.

Overdrive units are essentially pre-amps, or they tonally mimic pre-amps by increasing the pre-volume of a guitar's signal. Pre-amp units fulfil the same function as an amp's 'pre' control – boosting the signal before the later amplification stage. This family of effects also now includes pedals designed to create tuneable feedback.
Used by: Eddie Van Halen, Lars Ulrich and most Heavy Metal players
Classic models: *Ibanez Tube Screamer/Boss Overdrive*

Drenched in sweat, Gaz Coombes looks down at his impressive array of pedals.

Wah-Wah

This onomatopoeic effect is probably the most famous of pedals. Wah-Wahs were pioneered by Jimi Hendrix and electronics wizard Jim Dunlop, who built the pedals to Hendrix's specifications. They feature a rotary tone potentiometer, or 'pot', similar to a guitar's tone control. This is controlled by a pedal based on the design of a car's accelerator pedal (a similarity that is one of the basic appeals of pedals – putting your foot to the floor), which boosts different frequencies in a round swoop to create the 'wah-ing' effect. At full tilt, Wah-Wah adds searing treble to solos; if moved rapidly up and down, it can make the guitar 'talk'. On the Stone Roses' *Fool's Gold*, John Squire's 'wah-wah-ed' riff led to a huge revival in wah. If you're feeling lazy, auto-wahs can do the wah-ing for you, without you having to wiggle your foot.

A classic pedal – the Jim Dunlop 'Cry Baby' Wah-Wah.

Used by: Hendrix, John Squire, Clapton, Steve Vai
Classic models: *Jim Dunlop Cry Baby*

Treble boosts and EQ's

These two effects alter the tone of your guitar. Treble boosts add biting top for solos, while EQ's can shift the whole tonal balance of your sound.

Harmonizers and Octavers

These bizarre beasts add harmonies and/or notes that are one or two octaves below the actual note you're playing.

An MXR Blue Box harmonizer.

Used by: Jimmy Page
Classic models: *MXR Blue Box*

Compressors and Noise Gates

Despite the fact that these pedals don't seem to make much difference to a guitar's sound, they are actually very practical and widely used. Compressors even out the peaks and troughs in a guitar signal's volume, ensuring that a solo is as loud as a chord. They are often used in solos to increase the sustain of notes, and when employed in sequence after other pedals, they can even out any sudden changes in volume.

Noise Gates simply cut out unwanted noise from other pedal units or the guitar. Their 'threshold' level can be adjusted so that they only start to operate when the signal falls below a certain point.

Guitar Gear: Getting The Best From Your Pedals

Effects pedals are easy to use, but there are a few points to bear in mind for easy operation.

- **A failing battery, usually indicated by a dim LED light, will give a poorer sound quality and a lower output level than a fresh one.**

- **Most pedals stop using 'juice' from the battery when they are not plugged in. With this in mind, you should always unplug your jack leads from pedals when not using them for a long period.**

- **Batteries are fine as a source of power for Distortion and Overdrive units. Some manufacturers claim that vintage effects work best with vintage zinc batteries rather than modern alkaline ones, but this could simply be a marketing ploy. Different effects pedals use up different amounts of power; but as a general rule, digital units eat up the most. They can be powered up with individual adaptor units or specially made pedal containers, with a routed power supply for each pedal from only one plug. BOSS make a popular multi-effects panel like this.**

- **Using several pedals in sequence can create a lot of 'noise'. A Noise Gate unit will cut this out and only allow sound through its 'gate' when you're actually playing.**

- **If you're using a whole series of pedals, it's a good idea to place units that create large leaps in volume, such as Distortion or Overdrive, in a late position in the sequence, i.e. closest in the chain to your amp.**

DISTORTION PEDAL

If you're an electric guitar player with an amp, it's hard to resist the temptation of stomping on a Distortion pedal.

Here's a detailed look at how to use one of the most common electric guitar effects in rock music – a Distortion pedal. They may be called different names on different models, but the features of this BOSS DS-1 are relatively generic to all Distortion, Overdrive and Fuzz pedals.

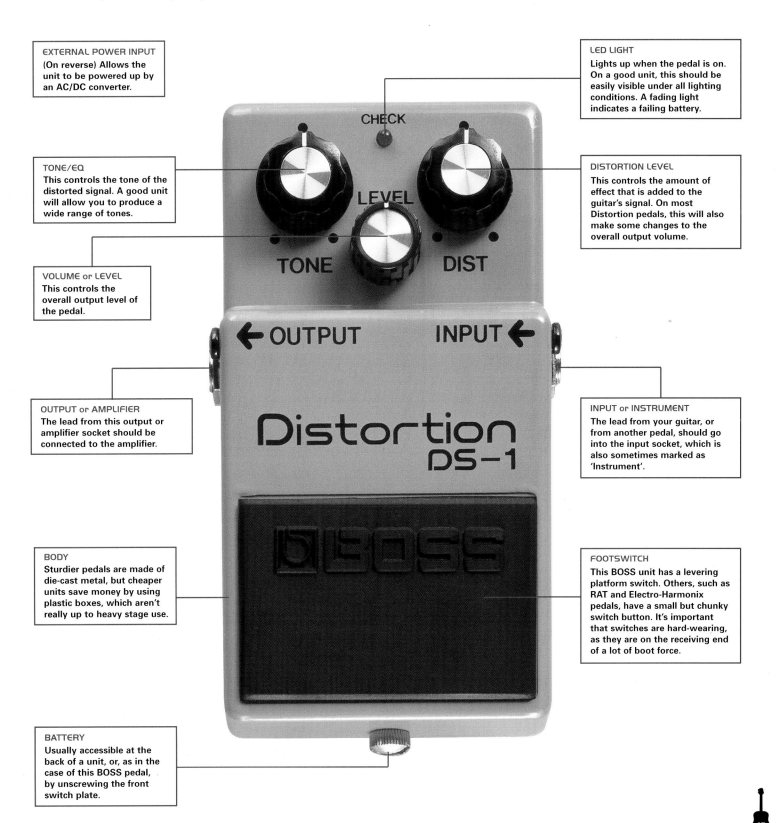

EXTERNAL POWER INPUT
(On reverse) Allows the unit to be powered up by an AC/DC converter.

LED LIGHT
Lights up when the pedal is on. On a good unit, this should be easily visible under all lighting conditions. A fading light indicates a failing battery.

TONE/EQ
This controls the tone of the distorted signal. A good unit will allow you to produce a wide range of tones.

DISTORTION LEVEL
This controls the amount of effect that is added to the guitar's signal. On most Distortion pedals, this will also make some changes to the overall output volume.

VOLUME or LEVEL
This controls the overall output level of the pedal.

OUTPUT or AMPLIFIER
The lead from this output or amplifier socket should be connected to the amplifier.

INPUT or INSTRUMENT
The lead from your guitar, or from another pedal, should go into the input socket, which is also sometimes marked as 'Instrument'.

BODY
Sturdier pedals are made of die-cast metal, but cheaper units save money by using plastic boxes, which aren't really up to heavy stage use.

FOOTSWITCH
This BOSS unit has a levering platform switch. Others, such as RAT and Electro-Harmonix pedals, have a small but chunky switch button. It's important that switches are hard-wearing, as they are on the receiving end of a lot of boot force.

BATTERY
Usually accessible at the back of a unit, or, as in the case of this BOSS pedal, by unscrewing the front switch plate.

TUNING WITH HARMONICS

The second part of our tuning guide; how to tune with harmonics, a very useful and precise method.

Relative tuning, as described on pages 40-41, is the most common quick-fix tuning method. However, you may have noticed that it can be difficult to match the sound of an 'open' unfretted string with a fretted note. Even if the notes are identical, they have different kinds of sounds. (In fact, a lot of the art of good guitar playing involves combining the different qualities of open and fretted strings in ways that complement each other.) Fortunately, there is a method of tuning that uses notes with an identical clarity of tone – tuning with harmonics. Combining this method with relative tuning is the best way to get in tune.

STEP 1

First, you need to be able to make a harmonic. We'll begin with one on string 6. Rest the tip of the 1st finger of your left hand on string 6, directly over fret 7 – not behind or in front of it, but exactly over the fretwire. Do not actually fret the string, just rest the finger on it. Play the string with your right hand and then lift your finger away. You should hear the harmonic. It will be easy to hear on an acoustic, but you should turn up your amp if you're using an electric.

STEP 2

Now that you've learnt the technique, try to make the harmonic found over the 5th fret of string 6. It's quieter and a little trickier than the 7th fret harmonic. As in our guide to relative tuning on pages 40-41, we'll begin by assuming that string 6 is roughly in tune. Play the harmonic with your 1st finger, lightly resting the tip directly over the fret as in Step 1.

STEP 3

While this note is ringing, use your 3rd finger to play the harmonic over the 7th fret of string 5, in exactly the same way as before, and start to tune string 5. As the notes come closer together, you should hear a 'wave' effect created by the vibrations of the two harmonics being out of synch with each other. As you tune string 5, you should hear that the oscillations of the wave get slower the closer the two notes are to each other in pitch. When the two notes are in tune, the wave effect should disappear. If you carry on raising the pitch of the string, as it gets sharper (i.e. higher than the desired note), the wave will gradually get faster too. Think of this wave as a naturally occurring tuning aid.

STEP 4

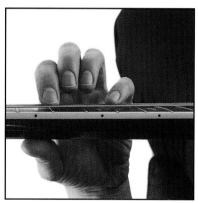

Repeat this process for string 4 by tuning its fret 7 harmonic to string 5's fret 5 harmonic. Play both together, then listen for the 'wave' as the notes synch together when you tune string 4.

Right: Harmonics at the 5th, 7th and 12th frets, with identical notes joined by red arrows.

String 2 open (circled in red) is the same as the 6th string's fret 7 harmonic, and string 1 open (circled in red) is the same as the 5th string's 7th fret harmonic.

Once you've learnt how to tune according to this method, you'll find that, like relative tuning, it's just as effective performed in the other direction, i.e. from the first string down.

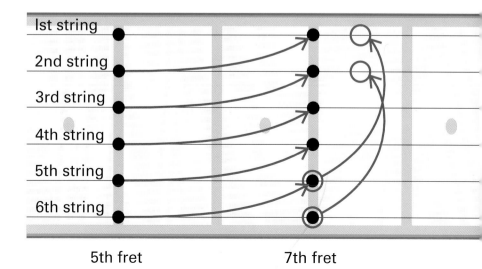

1st string
2nd string
3rd string
4th string
5th string
6th string

5th fret   7th fret

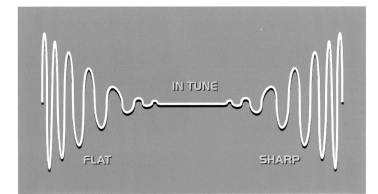

This is a diagrammatical representation of the 'wave' effect created by harmonics as they come into tune – a natural tuning aid. As the two notes converge, the wave slows down; it disappears when the notes are identical. This effect is audible when tuning fretted and open strings, but it is far clearer when using harmonics. In fact, it's the standard tuning method used by bass players, as listening to the tuning wave of harmonics is far easier than trying to discern the tuning of very low notes.

STEP 5

Repeat this process for string 3, by matching its fret 7 harmonic with string 4's fret 5 harmonic.

STEP 6

As in relative tuning, string 2 is different. You can't directly match any string 2 harmonics with those on string 3, but you can tune an open string 2 to the 6th string's fret 7 harmonic – they should be the same note.

STEP 7

Now play the 1st string's 7th fret harmonic with the 2nd string's fret 5 harmonic, and tune string 1 accordingly. As a final check, play the 5th string's fret 7 harmonic – it should be the same note as the open string 1 note (E).

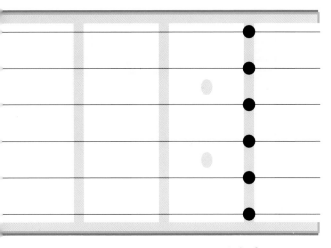

12th fret

WHAT IS A HARMONIC?

Harmonics are bell-like tones that can be produced by playing strings that have been 'stopped', but not fretted, with your left hand. They occur all over the strings, but are most noticeable at points that represent even divisions of the string: half its length, one quarter of its length, three-quarters of its length, etc. These are called 'nodes', and they are still points in-between the two vibrating lengths of the string.

The harmonic over the 12th fret of every string is always an octave up from the open string. Why? Because it occurs at the exact half-way point on a string. The 7th fret harmonic occurs at a quarter of a string's length.

The most commonly used harmonics are found over the 5th, 7th, 12th, 17th and 19th frets; the ones over frets 7 and 12 are the loudest and easiest to play. If your guitar has 24 frets (2 x 12 = 24), you'll find further harmonics over the 24th fret.

Harmonics have many uses; they're the best type of note to use with an electronic tuner, as the clean and pure tone that they provide is easy for the tuner to measure. They can also be incorporated into solos or riffs to add unusual textures to songs. The two most famous harmonics in rock are probably the two notes at the beginning of the Jimi Hendrix track *Stone Free*. It begins with the 12th fret harmonics on the 6th and then the 4th strings. See if you can recognize the pure, bell-like sound of the harmonics that feature in both The Edge's and Jonny Greenwood's playing.

Playing the 12th fret harmonic on the 6th string – an octave above the open string note.

ECHOES AND WAVES

A look at the space-creating sounds of Echo and Reverb, and the weird and wonderful world of waves.

By using Echo, Reverb or the 'wave' group of effects, a guitarist can really play around with his or her sound. Employed subtly, these effects can add a little tonal colour to chords or lead lines, but if used excessively, they can create unearthly sounds and textures that you wouldn't believe came from a guitar.

Echo and Reverb

Reverb, short for reverberation, was the first guitar effect to be created. It was developed in early recording studios by passing a signal through a metal plate suspended on springs. Known as Plate Reverb, this mimicked the 'splashing' effect of sound bouncing off walls in a large room or hall. Elvis' first recordings at Sun Studios in Memphis are saturated with this effect. It sounded so good when added to a guitar that Reverb Trays were integrated into guitar amplifiers. These create a similar effect to Plate Reverb by passing the amplified signal through a suspended spring (the effect is known as Spring Reverb). It's a common feature of many amp combos, but you can also get pedals that do the same job.

Reverb adds an artificial sense of space to a guitar. Many

A Boss DD-3 – a versatile delay unit with a 'hold' function.

players like to switch it on for solos, then off again for chords, and it's great for clean, twangy riffs (Blondie's *Atomic* or *The James Bond Theme*, for example). A short reverberation time simulates the sound of a small room, while a long reverberation time simulates a large hall, and so on. Digital Reverb units have a whole range of settings that mimic the sounds of many different sized spaces and the tonal qualities of different sound-reflective surfaces.

Echo adds texture to a solo, excitement to a riff and atmospherics to songs. It repeats the sound you are making, and by playing along with these repeats you can build up riffs out of an echoed pattern. The Edge, for one, has made an entire career out of rhythmic, echoed riffs, while Jonny Greenwood and Nick McCabe are both exponents of the Reverb and Echo effects, which are often cleverly used together. Graham Coxon used a medium length echo to add texture to his solo on *Beetlebum*. A short repeat creates the 'slap-back' effect that defined the guitar sounds of the 'Fifties and early 'Sixties. A very short echo produces an effect called ADT, or Automatic Double Tracking, a technique pioneered by The Beatles.

Longer repeat times add a more spacey effect – with a long echo time, it's even possible to jam along with yourself. The units themselves are often called Delays rather than Echoes because that's literally what they do – delay the signal before allowing you to play it as many times as you want.

Tape Echo

Tape Echo units produce a lot of hiss and noise, but the amplification involved in the unit and the analogue technology give a very warm and tonally rich sound that some players love. In fact, some sophisticated digital delays have a special function that mimics the sound of old Tape Echo units. The original early Tape

Brian May of Queen, known for his use of Tape Echo.

Echo effects units, such as the Watkins Echoplex or Copycat, simply feature a loop of tape that passes over one recording head and a series of playback heads. Choosing how many heads you hear selects the number of repeats; then, altering the speed of the tape varies the length of time between these repeats. These Echo units added a distinctive bounce to Hank Marvin's twanging in the 'Sixties, while Queen's Brian May used a customized Tape Echo machine to construct a whole song (*Brighton Rock*) out of long echoed parts, as did Pink Floyd.

Used by: Hank Marvin, Brian May, Dave Gilmour, The Edge

Classic Models: *Watkins/WEM Copycat Echoplex*

Analogue Echo

A circuit board imitator of Tape Echo, an Analogue Echo unit uses a series of transistors that act like a sequence of 'buckets', passing the inputted signal onto each other in the series. The repeats or echoes degrade in sound quality as they go on, producing an appealing softness of sound.

Used by: Will Sergeant (Echo and the Bunnymen) and many others

Classic Models: *Electro-Harmonix Echo/Boss D2/Roland Space Echo*

Danelectro's Analogue Echo pedal.

Digital Delay

These units digitally duplicate the original sound and repeat it as often as required without any loss in sound quality. Many Digital Delay pedals have a 'hold' function. This can be used to give a basic sampling effect by holding the delayed noise and playing it every time the pedal is depressed. Rack models are a standard feature of all studios and many also appear on stage set-ups.

Used by: Graham Coxon, Jonny Greenwood and many others

Classic Models: *BOSS DD-3*

The 'wave' group

Chorus, Flange and Phase have their origins in old reel-to-reel tape recording – George Martin frequently used these wave effects with The Beatles. While 'vari-speeding' a take (speeding up and

A GD foot pedal combining Chorus, Flange and Volume.

slowing down the tape while recording), a sound engineer could slightly shift the tape machine's magnetic recording heads, producing a 'wave' effect. Shifting the heads around slowly produced a 'phased' effect – a classic example of this effect can be heard on the 'Sixties smash, *Itchycoo Park* by The Small Faces. Analogue foot pedal versions produce these effects by passing the signal through a wave of noise that they generate. Digital units work like Digital Delays, copying the signal and shifting this repeat in and out of phase with the original signal in a modulating wave pattern.

The difference between Phase, Flange and Chorus lies in the speed of the delay and the shape of the modulating wave. Phase is a slow modulation, Flange is a similar modulation with an edge (called a flange) to the wave, and Chorus is a faster, shallower wave. Analogue units tend to make a lot of 'pink' noise which might be undesirable when you're not playing, but this can be removed with a Noise Gate unit, as featured on page 44. Then again, some players like this unmistakable 'whooshing' noise.

Studio-quality Digital Delay units have the ability to produce all of these effects, with depth and speed controls to alter the sound of the modulation. A touch of a wave effect can transform an ordinary sounding riff into an extraordinary one – think of the intro to Nirvana's *Come As You Are*, which has a little Chorus added, or the riff to Manic Street Preachers' *If You Tolerate This...*, which creates its chilling, antiseptic feel by clever use of a slow wave effect.

Chorus

The name Chorus comes from the Greek term for several voices singing in unison, and that's what this effect appears to do – make a single instrument sound like a couple. Digital units duplicate the original signal and repeat it fractionally later with a gently modulated wave, creating a relatively subtle thickening effect.

A Uni-Vibe foot pedal that combines Chorus and Vibrato.

Chorus adds a shimmering brightness to chords, a sheen to solos and riffs, and is often used with acoustic guitars to give a live or recorded sound greater prominence. Listen to Smiths era Johnny Marr, The Police, or the sound of The Pretenders from any year. The Beatles and the Beach Boys used to create a Chorus guitar effect by passing their amps' signal through Leslie speakers – speakers originally designed for Hammond organs that actually rotate, producing the whirring effect that is synonymous with the Hammond organ. Kurt Cobain used a little fast Chorus on the guitar solos on *Nevermind* to lift them above the rest of the band in the mix.

Used by: Kurt Cobain, Johnny Marr, The Pretenders
Classic Models: *BOSS CE-2/Electro-Harmonix Small Clone/Jim Dunlop Uni-Vibe/Ibanez Chorus*

Phaser

Using a Phaser produces a zany, psychedelic noise. Phase is hard to use subtly, so it is often employed in a tongue-in-cheek, kitsch kind of way.
Used by: Super Furry Animals, Small Faces, Supergrass, Hawkwind
Classic Models: *Electro-Harmonix Small Stone/ Colorsound Phaser*

MXR Flanger

Flanger

This produces an almost sinister effect. It was at one time the trademark sound of Siouxsie and the Banshees guitarist John McGeoch, who used it on arpeggio riffs or acoustic slashes. Fast Flange can sound great on solos, a trick Jon Spencer (of the Blues Explosion) sometimes uses.
Used by: Pavement, Jon Spencer, John McGeoch (Banshees, Magazine and PIL), Sonic Youth, Jimi Hendrix, Robin Guthrie (Cocteau Twins)
Classic Models: *MXR Flanger/Electro-Harmonix Electric Mistress*

Vibrato/Tremolo

These replicate the Vibrato effects that were once an integral part of old amp combos like the Fender Twin. Essentially, the guitar signal is broken up into a pulse, the depth and speed of which can be controlled by the unit. In fact, these effects should be called Tremolos, which implies a pulsing in volume, while Vibrato means a rapid alteration of pitch – so those whammy bars called tremolo arms should actually be called vibratos! Psychedelia again was responsible for combining Vibrato units with stereo panning devices and Phasers, so as the signal pulses and modulates, it is thrown from one amplifier to another across stage.

A Jim Dunlop Tremolo unit, with a design similar to a Wah-Wah pedal.

A classic Vibrato guitar riff is the lead line to Bruce Springsteen's *Born To Run*. Ubiquitous on 'Fifties and 'Sixties guitar tracks by Link Wray and Duane Eddy, its spooky sound is frequently used by both Massive Attack and Portishead. On The Smiths' *How Soon Is Now*, Johnny Marr created an entire guitar track from the rhythmic pulse of vibrato'd chords.
Used by: Johnny Marr, Link Wray, Placebo, Nirvana
Classic Models: *Colorsound Vibrasonic/Schaller Vibrato/'Flying Pan'*

A ZOOM 505, from the company that currently lead the market in multi-effects units.

Multi-effects

There has been a huge boom in the last few years in the quality and use of digital multi-effects units. These allow you to use different combinations of Overdrive, Chorus, Delay, Flange, Wah, or whatever you want, at a fraction of what buying all the units individually would cost. This used to be offset by the fact that each individual effect might not sound as great as an individual pedal, but now they all tend to have adjustable parameters (such as tone, volume, or depth) for each type of effect. They double up as excellent multi-effects units for home recording.
Classic Models: *ZOOM/Boss ME30*

DIGITAL DELAY PEDAL

For adding a sense of space to any guitar line, or atmospherics to a solo, most players opt for this effect – a Delay pedal.

Echo or Delay units are used by many guitarists, including Jonny Greenwood, Graham Coxon and The Edge. Here we look at a Digital Delay unit that is regarded as a very reliable and versatile model – the

BOSS DD-3. It has some features in common with the Distortion unit featured on page 45, and, although specific names differ, the functions remain broadly the same for different models of Delays.

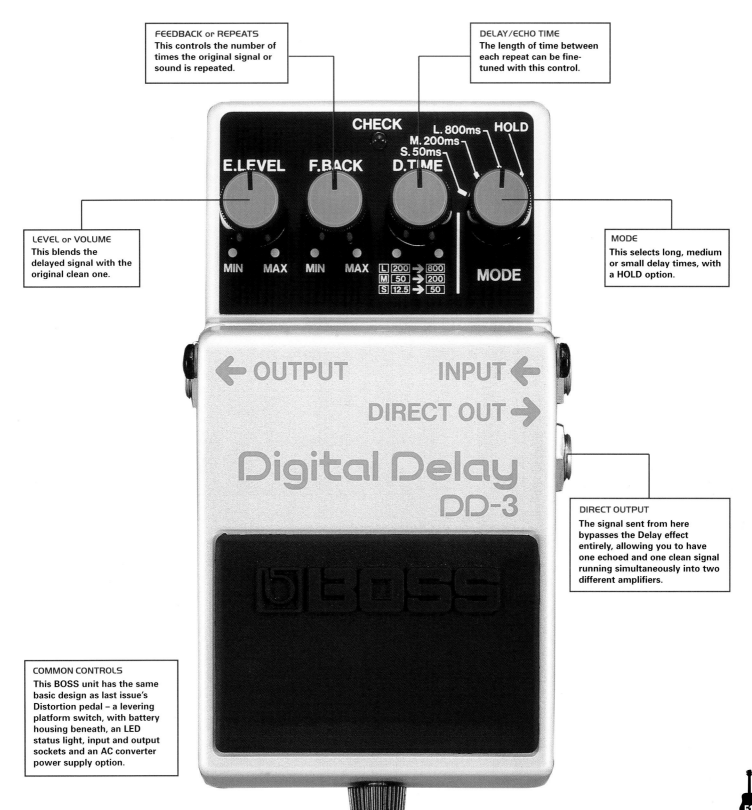

FEEDBACK or REPEATS
This controls the number of times the original signal or sound is repeated.

DELAY/ECHO TIME
The length of time between each repeat can be fine-tuned with this control.

LEVEL or VOLUME
This blends the delayed signal with the original clean one.

MODE
This selects long, medium or small delay times, with a HOLD option.

DIRECT OUTPUT
The signal sent from here bypasses the Delay effect entirely, allowing you to have one echoed and one clean signal running simultaneously into two different amplifiers.

COMMON CONTROLS
This BOSS unit has the same basic design as last issue's Distortion pedal – a levering platform switch, with battery housing beneath, an LED status light, input and output sockets and an AC converter power supply option.

ON THE CASE

From the cheap and cheerful to the most serious status symbol, we look at some of the different types of cases and stands available.

Whatever the quality, type or value of guitar you own, it should be kept in the toughest and best-quality case you can afford. Buying a case at the same time as the guitar tends to save money. Once there were only two kinds of case: a cloth bag or wooden hard case, but over the last few years, a wide variety of designs have appeared that help to keep a guitar safe while making it easier to carry. In the way it evokes the idea of 'have-guitar-will-travel', the guitar case plays its own part in the mythology of the guitar. And, of course, an open guitar case doubles up nicely as a busker's collection box.

Soft cases

Usually made of vinyl or cloth, soft cases may make a guitar easier to carry, but they won't protect the instrument from any kind of knocks. However, they are definitely better than no protection at all.

Vinyl bags are susceptible to tearing, so some makes use a Teflon-based fabric, which makes this less likely to occur. But although this material is both tough and rainproof, it can't cushion any blows. So, if you're buying a soft case, look for bags that have at least some degree of padding. If the case is closed with a zip, make sure the zip is strongly attached, since this will often take most of the wear and tear.
Price guide: £5 – £12 approx.

Gig bags

A deluxe descendant of the soft case, gig bags are an absolute boon. They are highly portable, durable and lightweight, which is an important consideration if your guitar is an electric that already weighs a fair amount. Their most attractive feature is the different types and positions of both handles and carrying straps available on any one bag. Some even have rucksack-type back straps. Basically, any guitar is a cumbersome thing to carry, so the more carrying options the better. Anyone who has navigated turnstiles on the tube or tried paying the fare on a bus ride while carrying a guitar will tell you that it's a bonus to be able to have both hands free. Good gig bags have a wide shoulder or back strap with

A Wings padded and multi-handled bag.

Johnny Marr in The Smiths' heyday, carefully packing his beloved Gibson ES335 away in its hard case.

friction pads to keep it in place. Made of tough, padded fabric, they offer a reasonable level of protection against the minor knocks your guitar might experience while you're on the move. Another bonus feature is reinforced, closeable pockets; manufacturers have finally realized that guitarists need to keep some essential equipment with their guitar at all times, such as a set of spare strings, a notebook, plectrums and maybe a lead or two.
Price guide: £12 – £40 approx.

Hard cases

Hard cases are good enough to protect your guitar from most mishaps, and are usually made of covered plywood.

The most important feature of a hard case is that it fits the guitar closely and that it is cushioned enough to prevent any movement of the guitar inside the case. There are cases available that are designed to fit every shape of instrument.

When buying your guitar, see if you can get a hard case thrown in for a minimal extra amount, as this will

A Yamaha acoustic in a close-fitting hard case.

invariably be cheaper than buying one afterwards. Look for strong hinges – cheap alloy fittings that are badly attached will work loose and break with regular use. Cases often have an internal holder under the neck support, which is a great place for strings.

It's worth thinking about the handle because a hard case adds a little weight to your load. Hard-moulded plastic handles can cause hand-ache, even before you get to your destination, so look for padded leather or soft foam handles for comfort. The metal fittings on a hard case are important too. Sadly, the locks on hard cases are often flimsy and wouldn't deter a determined thief; realistically speaking, their main job when locked is to add strength and prevent the case from suddenly springing open. Hinges, too, need to be strong and well designed, as cheap alloy fittings can become misshapen with regular use and can work loose if badly attached. Fender's own-brand hard cases tend to be rectangular, while Gibson's are guitar-shaped.

Price guide: £30 – £40, and upwards

Moulded cases

Built of one-piece moulded plastic or glass fibre, these hard cases are extremely resilient and tough. Lighter than conventional hard cases, they are also a good alternative to the heavier and far more expensive flight cases.

A Kinsman vacuum-moulded case for an acoustic guitar.

Guitar Gear: Cases
Safety and security

• **Permanently marking your name and address on a hard case – either with a stencil and spray paint, or marker pen – will both act as some kind of deterrent to thieves and make your case easily identifiable. Your local police station can label both a guitar and its case with an invisible identification mark, which will make recovery easier.**

• **Insurers will be more likely to pay up for any damage to a guitar if the instrument was in a decent case at the time. (As well as all the advantages of expert advice, membership of the Musicians Union includes automatic equipment insurance up to a limited amount.)**

• **If travelling by plane, ask if you can take your guitar as hand luggage, or, if it has to go in the hold, plaster your hard case with FRAGILE stickers.**

• **Excess string length protruding from your machine heads can poke through vinyl or cloth cases, so trim it off with wire cutters (see page 21).**

• **If you have a second-hand case that is slightly larger than your guitar, jam the gaps with foam or some similar protective material.**

• **Guitars with Strat or locking-type tremolo units should always have their tremolo arm removed in the appropriate manner before being shut away in a hard case, as few cases allow for the depth of a tremolo arm when closed.**

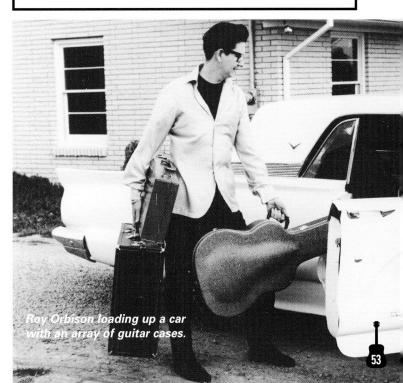

Roy Orbison loading up a car with an array of guitar cases.

Flight cases

Flight cases offer the ultimate protection. Designed to withstand all knocks – bar a plane landing on them – they are made of wood and metal, with a large reinforced metal trim. The guitar sits in a foam template and the case is closed with rotary clamping locks. Inevitably, due to the materials used and the degree of reinforcement, they are very heavy and therefore impractical for most players; hence, they are a kind of status symbol, as they indicate that you are successful enough to afford to pay someone else to carry them!

A tough rectangular case for an electric guitar.

Stands

Although it is advisable to put a guitar back in its case whenever possible, this isn't always practical and, in truth, one of the best ways to develop confidence and ease in your playing is to have your guitar to hand at all times. Hendrix is famous for virtually never putting his Strat down, and according to Chas Chandler, his manager, he would quite often be found frying eggs for breakfast with it still slung around his neck.

Just leaving a guitar leaning upright or against an amp can be extremely risky. Stands – simple free-standing devices that can also put your guitar on display – are the solution.

Basic models

Guitar stands are usually designed as a folding tripod with an adjustable neck support. There are light, cheap models for home use and tougher models for touring and stage work. Stands are a good option for professional guitarists who use more than one instrument during a live set and therefore need to be able to change guitar with the minimum of fuss.
Price guide: £10 – £30 approx.

A basic JHS guitar stand.

Amp-mounted holders

Most electric guitar players tend to leave their instrument in a precarious position, propped up against their amp. An amp-mounted holder removes the

String Swing's ingenious amp-mounted guitar holder.

risk of accident as it holds the guitar safely in place by supporting it around the neck.

Wall-mounted holders

There are also space-saving guitar holders that can be permanently fixed to a wall. These holders, such as the type seen suspending the guitar of your dreams in guitar shops, brace the guitar just below the headstock.

A String Swing wall-mounted holder.

Multiple guitar racks are really the domain of the professional player who has enough guitars to justify having one. Before they became internationally successful, Sonic Youth's twin guitarists, Thurston Moore and Lee Renaldo, would simply have empty tea-crates loaded with an array of de-tuned guitars.

Jake Vegas of Joe Whitney's Tropics of Cancer, putting a hard case to another good use – collecting the cash when busking.

CAPOS

A strange-looking device that is actually a quick and easy way to change the key of any guitar part.

You may have noticed odd clamp-like devices placed around the lower frets of guitars by players in performance. These are capos, short for *capotasto*, which translates literally from Italian as 'head of the touch', meaning the beginning of the string. They act as a temporary bar across all the strings and can be fitted at any fret. The open strings with a capo fitted are pitched higher than before. Players use capos when they want to raise the pitch of any particular part without having to change their fingering. Capos are essentially a bar with a rubber or cork surface that is clamped onto the neck of a guitar.

Types of capo

There are two basic types of capo: one uses a fabric or elasticated strap, which is fastened to a hole or slot after it has been looped around a guitar's neck, to control the tension; the other is a mechanical, clamping capo, some of which can retain a fixed tension between one use and the next. The main consideration when choosing a capo, however, has to be your guitar's fretboard. A flat fretboard needs a flat-surfaced capo, while a curved one requires a curved capo. Both designs should also match the string type in size and strength.

Tonality

Having a fret as a top nut, or 'zero' fret, also changes the tonality of the strings. Open strings and fretted strings normally sound different because of the difference between the material of the top nut and the fretwire. But when using a capo, all strings are, effectively, fretted and so produce a uniformly bright tone.

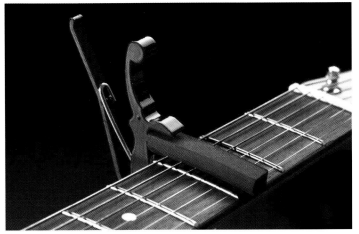
A Kyser metal clamp-style capo at the 3rd fret of a guitar.

A stretch-fabric capo, displayed (not fitted) on a guitar neck.

HOW TO FIT A CAPO

1. Fitting a capo is relatively easy. Tune your guitar as normal, either by using the relative tuning method (pages 40-41) or with a tuner.

2. Place the 'pad' of the capo on the strings, directly behind the desired fret.

3. Adjust the capo's tension so that it is as tight as possible around the neck of the body, and then clamp the capo down.

4. Play each string and listen for 'buzzing'. If any of the strings do buzz, then refit the capo nearer to the fret or try increasing the tension.

Tuning

When a capo is on, you should re-tune your guitar using the relative tuning method, treating the capo as the top nut. Due to the pressure that is applied to the strings, the need to re-tune once the capo is in place and after it has been removed is an inherent drawback. However, with a good model and a well set-up guitar, it shouldn't take too long.

A GUIDE TO TREMOLO SYSTEMS

Tremolos, which allow you to drop and raise note pitch, can be an integral part of a player's style. Here we explore a range of tremolo designs.

You may be at the stage where you are still focusing on your left and right techniques, and won't be using a tremolo (or 'trem' for short) as an integral part of your playing. However, tremolos are a standard feature on most solid-bodied electrics, and even guitars without tremolos already fitted can be customized relatively easily to incorporate one, so it's a good idea to know how trems work, how to use them and how to disable them (if you so wish).

Tremolos are really an extension of string bending, but they allow you to drop as well as raise note pitch, and whole chords as well as individual notes can be given that distinctive twang. Trems are sometimes incorrectly called vibratos, but the terms have become inter-changeable through misuse.

A close-up of a Fender Stratocaster's 'Synchronized Tremolo'.

Standard Stratocaster 'Synchronized Tremolo'

Since it first went on sale in 1954, the Stratocaster has been fitted with a patented 'Synchronized Tremolo'. A whole range of Surfcasters and assorted bizarre guitars with tremolos sprang up in its wake, but the Strat's trem proved to be the most workable design.

Inevitably, the popularity of the Strat led to its trem design becoming one of the most commonly manufactured and copied systems, both by Fender and other guitar makers.

On a Strat tremolo system, the strings are anchored in a metal block just under the bridge assembly, which is held in place by six screws that

Hendrix used his tremolo to wrench soaring high notes from his Strat.

bore directly into the wood of the guitar's body. Tightening these screws reduces any possible movement of the tremolo system. The tremolo arm is screwed into the bridge to the right of the bridge pieces; the stiffness of this arm depends on how tightly it is screwed in.

The strings have to pass up through the bridge from below, through six holes in the plate on the back of the guitar. Removing this plate reveals the surprisingly crude mechanics of the Fender tremolo – up to five large springs pull against the bridge at one end, anchored to a plate screwed directly into the body.
Used by: Eric Clapton, Richie Blackmore, Jimi Hendrix, Dave Gilmour, Hank Marvin, Yngwie Malmsteen, Buddy Guy and a host of other stars
Found on: *Stratocasters, most Strat copies*

Bigsby/Tailpiece tremolos

On these systems, the strings are anchored in a tailpiece – a brace that starts at the bottom of the guitar. When the trem arm is depressed, this tailpiece pole rotates slightly, reducing the strings' tension and therefore lowering their pitch. The trem arm is returned to its position – and string tension restored – by a crude single spring at its base. A variant on this was a plate behind the bridge instead of a trem arm, as used by Tony McPhee of The Groundhogs.
Used by: Brian Setzer (Stray Cats), Duane Eddy, Bernard Butler, Neil Young
Found on: *Gibson semi-acoustics, Gretsch, some Gibson SG's. Some early Fender Telecaster models were fitted with a similar spring-based set-up.*

Design drawbacks

Spring-based tremolos create one main problem – if used heavily, they can pull the guitar out of tune. To stay in tune, every string has to return to its original tension when the trem returns to its position. Friction and give in the springs make this problematic. Also, each string has three isolated lengths: from tuning machine to top nut, top nut to bridge, and from bridge saddle to string

Fender Stratocaster courtesy of Portobello Music. 13 All Saints Road. London W11 1HA.

anchor. The tension might not be equal in each length, and the nut and bridge saddles might provide resistance to strings moving across them (an effect known as 'binding'). To stay in tune, a string needs to travel freely without friction over these features.

Locking tremolo units

In the late 'Seventies, American guitar manufacturers Floyd Rose produced a tremolo system in response to a growing dissatisfaction with the Strat trem's tuning problems. Several innovations countered the old problems, such as string trees with lubricated wheels and top nuts designed to reduce friction. The biggest development was a locking top nut – clamping pads, tightened with Allen keys, prevented any movement of the strings above the headstock. This feature, however, necessitated 'fine tuners' on the bridge, since the ringing length of the string, once clamped, was no longer affected by the tuning machines. Locking top nuts were sometimes substituted by locking tuning machines, which also kept string tension constant.

The 'whammy bar' itself: a screw-in Strat-style tremolo arm.

Another improvement was a 'fulcrum' bridge, which pivoted on as fine a point as possible, preventing friction and allowing for a wide range of pitch variation with the trem arm. The area behind and below the bridge was often cut away to allow for even greater pitch variation.

The drawback of these locking systems is that they tend to look like small tanks, and larger units can hinder right hand movements and damping. Another disadvantage is that to de-tune or to drop any one string to a lower note involves undoing the string clamp, de-tuning, re-clamping and re-tuning.

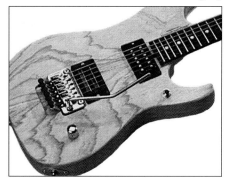

Washburn's hi-tech Nuno Bettencourt model with Floyd Rose tremolo system.

Used by: Eddie van Halen, Nuno Bettencourt (Extreme)
Models: *Floyd Rose, Schaller, Ibanez*
Found on: *Washburn, Jackson, Charvel, Ibanez*

Hybrid systems

In response to these drawbacks, new hybrid styles of tremolo systems have emerged. These have simpler fine tuning systems that don't require scalloped areas behind the bridge, and in some cases they have frictionless features that add tuning security to most models.

Some manufacturers are even now re-issuing vintage models with improved tremolo designs – the new standard USA Strat's smooth low-friction bridge saddles are a case in point, blending modern engineering improvements with traditional design.
Used by: Crispian Mills, Frank Black (Pixies) and most modern players
Found on: *'Series' Fender Guitars, Shecter, Ibanez and Strat*

Other designs

The demands of guitarists have lead to all kinds of innovations. For example, 'dropped D' tremolo systems are available that allow the 6th or 1st strings to be dropped and held in a lower tuning. A string bend common in country music led to the development of the 'B-bender' tremolo system (beloved of Jimmy Page), which affects only the 2nd string. The tremolo you use affects the kind of sounds that you can create.

Master of pyrotechnic solos that make full use of sophisticated tremolo systems – Eddie van Halen.

HOW TO USE A TREMOLO

There is a very good chance that you have a tremolo system on your guitar; here's how to get to grips with it.

Some players, such as Hank Marvin, keep the tremolo constantly in their hand, allowing it to rotate slightly as their picking hand moves around the strings. Others like it in a loose, passive position where it can be easily grasped for a specific part; a Strat-style trem can be screwed as tightly or loosely as desired.

Hold the tremolo arm loosely in the palm of your hand.

If you do want to use a trem as a natural part of your technique, the more you use one the less unnatural it will feel. Try adding slow downward tremolo bends to chords, or fast tremolo.

Pulling the arm up and away from the body raises the pitch of the strings; pressing it into the body of the guitar lowers the pitch.

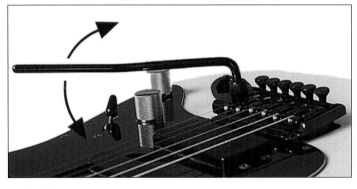

Tuning with a locking tremolo system

Tune your guitar as you would do normally with the top nut unlocked and fine tuners in a neutral/halfway position. Then lock the strings down gently with an Allen key. Stop tightening when the Allen screw won't turn without considerable force. Now re-tune – preferably with an electronic tuner – using the fine-tuning machines mounted on the bridge. Excessive tremolo use can cause tuning problems even with a locking system.

Disabling a tremolo

Removing the backplate on a Strat-type guitar reveals the springs that pull against the tremolo unit.

If you find that the trem is getting in the way while you are learning, you can simply remove the arm in the appropriate manner. Some right-hand techniques, such as palm damping, can be difficult with a tremolo on the guitar, as any pressure on the bridge will cause a change in pitch. On a Strat-type model, the trem can be disabled by screwing the six bridge fixing screws firmly down, preventing the trem from rocking at all. On a hybrid or Floyd Rose style system, it's a little trickier. Springs can be added to the tremolo anchor plate to increase resistance, and the bridge can be set up to minimize movement. However, it is important to note that these devices will affect the playability of the guitar in the form of its action – a crucial hardware subject that will be looked on pages 60-63.

On a guitar with a locking tremolo system, the guitar should be tuned as normal before gently clamping the strings down with the locking top nut (left). Tuning can then only be adjusted by using the fine tuners located on the bridge (right).

TOOLED UP

An overview of some of the most useful tools you need to keep your guitar in good working order.

Assembled here are some of those tools, which together make up an essential kit for an electric or acoustic player.

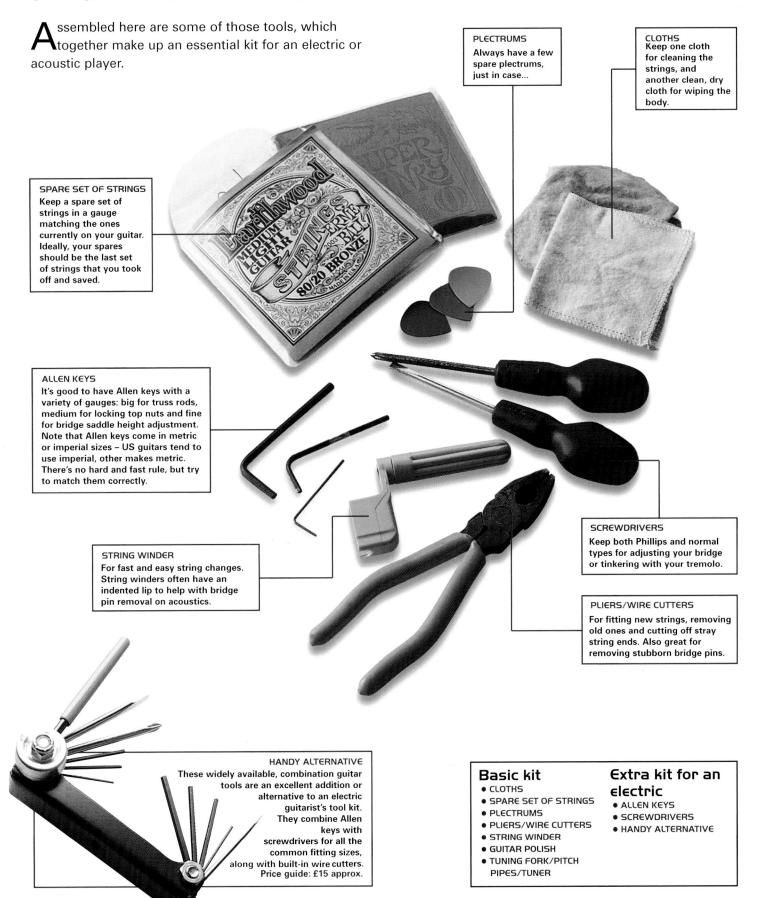

PLECTRUMS
Always have a few spare plectrums, just in case...

CLOTHS
Keep one cloth for cleaning the strings, and another clean, dry cloth for wiping the body.

SPARE SET OF STRINGS
Keep a spare set of strings in a gauge matching the ones currently on your guitar. Ideally, your spares should be the last set of strings that you took off and saved.

ALLEN KEYS
It's good to have Allen keys with a variety of gauges: big for truss rods, medium for locking top nuts and fine for bridge saddle height adjustment. Note that Allen keys come in metric or imperial sizes – US guitars tend to use imperial, other makes metric. There's no hard and fast rule, but try to match them correctly.

STRING WINDER
For fast and easy string changes. String winders often have an indented lip to help with bridge pin removal on acoustics.

SCREWDRIVERS
Keep both Phillips and normal types for adjusting your bridge or tinkering with your tremolo.

PLIERS/WIRE CUTTERS
For fitting new strings, removing old ones and cutting off stray string ends. Also great for removing stubborn bridge pins.

HANDY ALTERNATIVE
These widely available, combination guitar tools are an excellent addition or alternative to an electric guitarist's tool kit. They combine Allen keys with screwdrivers for all the common fitting sizes, along with built-in wire cutters. Price guide: £15 approx.

Basic kit
- CLOTHS
- SPARE SET OF STRINGS
- PLECTRUMS
- PLIERS/WIRE CUTTERS
- STRING WINDER
- GUITAR POLISH
- TUNING FORK/PITCH PIPES/TUNER

Extra kit for an electric
- ALLEN KEYS
- SCREWDRIVERS
- HANDY ALTERNATIVE

GUITAR SET-UP PART I: ACTION

Action, an essential part of every instrument's set-up, has a direct effect on its playability.

The Holy Grail of guitar action is a fast, or low, action. This has the strings set as close to the fretboard as possible, but still ringing cleanly when fretted at any point on the fretboard. A guitar that is set up like this requires the minimum physical effort to play, allowing the guitarist to indulge in fast left hand techniques and smooth chord changes. Action is created by many interdependent factors, so understanding it provides a real insight into the mechanics of guitar playing.

History of action

Like every other aspect of guitars, action has changed over the years. Manufacturers have to meet the demands of the majority of customers, so trends in action have matched fashions in music. In the 'Fifties

Bo Diddley and his custom-made 'box' guitar, set up for rhythmic chords rather than solos.

and 'Sixties, most solid-bodied electrics had relatively high action, needed for a fashionably twangy sound, and had little room for a fast action at the higher frets. Just as most electric guitarists now use a far finer gauge of string than they did when electrics were first manufactured (due to string bending and high-note solos becoming a standard part of guitar vocabulary), so both acoustic and electric players now expect to be able to solo easily at any point, resulting in a need for an easier and more adjustable action. The vogue for elaborate virtuoso lead soloing that emerged in the 'Seventies and 'Eighties accelerated this process.

Action for different styles

Within certain limits, the action that players prefer is largely determined by their playing style. Strings that are set relatively high require considerable strength to play, but give a strong tone with minimal risk of string buzz. Broadly speaking, steel string acoustics need to have higher action than solid-bodied electrics because of the heavier strings and the need for a greater natural resonance. For fast solo work, a low action is essential all the way up the neck, but rhythm players who play mainly root notes and bar chords are probably better off with a higher action than soloists might prefer. A notably high action is usually preferred for any kind of slide or bottleneck playing – a great technique that we look at later.

For players of Spanish guitars, the consistent height of the strings along the length of the fretboard, as well as the different playing style, means that action hardly applies in the steel string sense of the term.

Beginners with steel string guitars should ideally set up for

The 'Tun-o-matic' bridge of a Gibson Les Paul, easily adjustable for height.

a workable all-round action – low enough to make playing comfortable and chord changes easy, but without any buzzing of the strings.

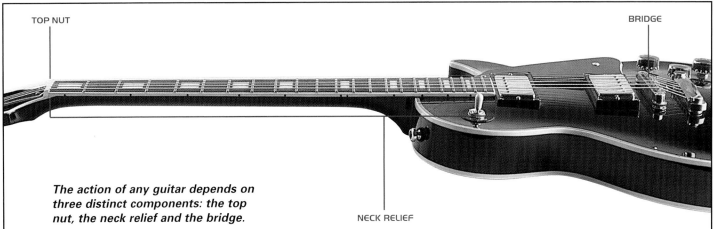

TOP NUT

BRIDGE

The action of any guitar depends on three distinct components: the top nut, the neck relief and the bridge.

NECK RELIEF

Gibson Les Paul courtesy of Portobello Music, 13 All Saints Road, London W11 1HA.

Action factors

Three factors affect a guitar's action (shown above). Both the top nut and the bridge directly affect the string height, while the neck relief affects the angle and curve of the fretboard.

Top nut

The first stage of a guitar's action occurs at the top nut. The crucial measurement is the distance between the bottom of the groove in the nut and the 'crown' of the 1st fret. This determines the height of the string above the fretboard at the headstock end. The strings should leave the nut at a height that is low enough for easy fretting around the lower frets, and high enough to prevent open strings from touching the frets when they vibrate (as this both deadens open string notes and creates unwanted buzzes). The nut has to match the 'camber' (the radial curve) of the fretboard.

Neck relief and the truss rod

Unlike the relatively low degree of stress created by nylon strings on Spanish guitars, the stress of the strings on a steel strung guitar, be it electric or acoustic, has a natural tendency to bow the neck by pulling it towards the body. Along with the hard woods specifically chosen for neck construction, this deforming stress is countered by the truss rod, an

adjustable metal bolt that is fitted inside the length of the neck and anchored at both the headstock and fretboard ends. The

The truss rod cover of a Gibson Les Paul removed for adjustment.

pull of the strings and the combined resistance of the neck's wood and truss rod create the lengthways curve of the neck, which is known as its relief.

There should be a slight, barely perceptible bow in a guitar neck to allow for the depth of vibration of the strings (called the amplitude), which is greatest at the centre of the sounding length of a string. Some players like the maximum degree of bowing, while others prefer the tightest possible truss rod adjustment. The tension of the truss rod affects the feel of the guitar – having a little give in the neck feels more comfortable and is less wearing on the left hand.

Cross-section of a Fender neck, showing the truss rod and the fretboard's camber.

The bridge

The height of the bridge, the bridge saddles or, on an acoustic, the bridge bone, is the final measurement. If the bridge is too low, strings that sound fine at the lower frets might buzz at the higher frets. If the bridge is set too high, it will make playing at the higher frets painful and difficult. Like the top nut, the bridge bone of an acoustic, or the individual saddle or combined bridge heights of an electric, has to have a curve that matches the camber of the fretboard.

The saddle and bridge of a Yamaha acoustic.

ADJUSTING YOUR ACTION

Here we show you how to alter the height of your bridge – the most straightforward adjustment you can make to a guitar's action.

Measuring string clearance at the 12th fret.

Thankfully, many manufacturers and shops set up their instruments to a good standard before they reach the public, but even so, you might wish to alter an instrument to suit your own needs and preference. A poor action, in which the strings are set so high off the fretboard that they require a great deal of physical force to fret – inflicting the 'cheese-wire effect' on fingers – is often a reason why many students get to a certain point in their playing and then find it difficult to progress. If this sounds familiar, compare the following measurements with those of your own guitar.

Between the crown of fret 12 and the bottom of a string
Electric: 1.3 mm – 2 mm (0.05 in – 0.08 in)
Acoustic: 2 mm – 2.8 mm (0.08 in – 0.11 in)

Between the crown of fret 1 and the bottom of a string
Electric: 0.25 mm – 0.50 mm (0.01 in – 0.02 in)
Acoustic: 0.35 mm – 0.65 mm (0.015 in – 0.03 in)

If your guitar's measurements are noticeably outside these guidelines, it could well benefit from a little attention. An easy solution would be to take it to a workshop to have it set up, which should cost between £20 and £40. However, you can take a few steps to improve the action for yourself, which can give you a real sense of satisfaction, and a better understanding of your instrument.

Adjusting the bridge on an electric

On a well-made guitar, the easiest and most sensible adjustment to make is to the height of the bridge. The bridge of an electric guitar is either adjustable for height string by string (as on Fender types with individual saddles), or with two side screws that determine the height of the whole bridge piece (as on Gibson types). Both can be adjusted with the strings still on, but make sure you slacken them off slightly before getting started.

A fine Allen key for individual bridge saddle adjustment.

Adjusting individual saddles

Adjust individual saddles either with a fine screwdriver or an Allen key, depending on the slot in the screw head – don't try to use a small screwdriver for an Allen key as you will burr the thread on the screws and

Adjusting the height of individual bridge saddles with an Allen key.

repeated adjustment will render them useless. Remember to mimic the camber (the radial curve of the fingerboard in the individual saddle heights) of the neck, if it has one. On guitars with a flat fretboard, remember that heavier gauge strings need marginally more clearance to ring without touching the frets.

Adjusting Gibson types

With a bridge that is adjustable by just the screws (as on a Gibson), screwing clockwise into the body will lower the bridge, while screwing anti-clockwise will raise it. This is made easier if the strings are slackened right off, which decreases downward pressure on the bridge. Screw incrementally, measuring in quarter turns; this way, if you overdo it, you can return the bridge to its previous level.

After every adjustment, re-tune and check how the guitar sounds. Fret the strings at high, low and middle fret positions, and check for any buzzes. Once you've adjusted the bridge to a sensible height, check that the strings don't touch the pick-ups when played at the upper frets; pick-up heights can be easily adjusted via their mounting screws.

Adjusting an acoustic

The action on an acoustic is a little trickier to tackle. The bridge on most steel strung acoustics has a separate bridge bone, which can be taken out easily once the strings have been slackened off or removed. To lower the action of the saddle, carefully sand down the flat bottom of the bone with a fine-grade sandpaper. Sanding the curved top of the bone is trickier, since you have to maintain a curvature that matches the camber of the neck and the required relative string heights. A good method is to wrap the sandpaper around the flat

An acoustic's bridge bone can be easily removed when the strings are taken off.

level surface of a brick, and gently rub the base of the bridge bone on the sandpaper in a circular motion to ensure even filing. Proceed with caution, removing a small amount at a time. Replacement bridge saddles are available from most guitar shops, but you should still take a great deal of care. (For bridge saddles with built-in transducer pick-ups, refer to your nearest guitar shop for advice.)

Once filed, refit the bone, string up again and check the sound of the strings. This laborious method of trial and error is the only way.

Top nut adjustment

You can adjust the top nut if it is really necessary, but in truth this is best left to a professional. Luthiers use fine files to achieve the optimum height. The slots have to be filed at a slight upward angle so that the strings leave the nut at its highest point. A downward angle in a top nut's groove can result in an unwanted sitar-like buzz when a string is played open.

Truss rod adjustment

If string height is within the given parameters but your strings buzz around the middle frets, adjusting your truss rod could rectify the problem. To check this, with a capo at the 1st fret and the strings held down at the

other end of the fretboard, measure the string clearance at the deepest point (the 7th or 8th fret). It should be between 0.15 mm – 0.50 mm (0.005 in – 0.020 in).

If you do need to adjust your truss rod, proceed with caution – modern instruments can recover from truss

Adjusting the truss rod of a Strat-type neck with an Allen key.

rod over-tension, but guitars with a variety of woods in the neck, or older truss rod fittings, can be ruined. Use the appropriate tool for the fitting – either an Allen key or a screwdriver. On some guitars, the truss rod is concealed under a plate on the headstock, or found at the base of the neck.

Helpful hints

- **To check all the measurements given in this feature, use a ruler with a measurement gauge that starts at the edge, or a graduated feeler gauge used for car maintenance.**

- **Ensure that you have on your guitar a fairly new set of strings, settled in and tuned, before taking any measurements or making adjustments.**

- **Don't try to use a conventional screwdriver to turn Allen screws as this will burr their thread, eventually rendering them useless. Individual Allen keys can be bought cheaply from most hardware shops.**

- **Heavier gauge strings cause more bowing of the neck relief, and so need more truss rod compensation than lighter ones.**

- **If you do feel that truss rod adjustment is necessary, proceed with caution. Tighten incrementally in quarter turns and re-check the relief with strings on and tuned.**

- **If your guitar's string height measurements are within the guidelines, don't be tempted to alter them for the sake of it.**

RINGING TRUE – A GUIDE TO INTONATION

A subtle and arcane art, involving string gauges and bridge settings, correct intonation can make a vital difference to your guitar's sound.

If a guitar had a bridge set absolutely parallel, you would find that many fretted notes were actually out of tune with their equivalent harmonics (see page 46). This would get worse the higher up the neck you went. Fretting strings higher up makes the angle at which they leave the bridge more acute, and this, along with string thickness, effectively shortens the vibrating length of a fretted string. As a result, the heavier strings require longer lengths to keep them in tune at the frets all the way up the neck. Conversely, the finer strings need shorter lengths.

To achieve this, each string needs its part of the bridge to be in a slightly different position. A look at the bridge of a steel string guitar reveals it to be set at an angle – not straight like the frets or top nut – to compensate for

the gradual change in string gauge. On an electric, the saddles will often appear to be in two sets of steps, from the 6th to the 4th strings, and from the 3rd to the 1st.

Electric intonation

When there were only a limited variety of string gauges available, electrics were built with fixed bridges. Cello-bodied jazz guitars had a wood or bone bridge piece

A Fender-type bridge with adjustable saddles. Notice how each string is set at a slightly different angle.

with compensatory lengths carved into them. However, the advent of different string gauges meant that the bridge saddles on electrics had to be adjustable. Higher fret access made similar demands on intonation as on action, and now most players would expect chords and notes played higher up the neck to be totally in tune with ones played in lower positions.

Acoustic intonation

On steel string acoustics, makers set the bridge bone at an angle at the manufacturing stage. Since this is a permanent fixture, there is a limited range of string gauges that will sound absolutely true all the way up the neck. This is less of a problem than you might think, because of the limited access to upper frets on an acoustic. However, the trend for cutaways on acoustics has led to more sophisticated bridges, which have different surfaces for each string cut into the bone in an approximation of separate saddles.

Good intonation

Intonation affects the overall resonance of an instrument – a guitar with good intonation rings true at every position, while one with poor intonation will always sound a little odd even if it appears to be in tune. In fact, correct tuning can be made difficult by bad intonation. Soloists frequently combine fretted notes with harmonics – George Harrison's solo on *Nowhere Man*, for example – and these should not clash. How concerned you are about it is up to you – Manchester band The Fall's early output is clearly played on guitars with bad intonation, as are several tracks by art-house legends The Velvet Underground.

George Harrison taking time out from the 'Fab Four' to clean up his Gretsch and check its bridge.

ADJUSTING YOUR INTONATION

How to adjust an electric guitar's intonation – a practical and satisfying way of improving its sound.

Adjusting the intonation on an acoustic is difficult and, realistically, should be left to a professional. However, modern bridge design makes adjusting the intonation of an electric very easy. Since this will help to train your 'musical ear', we thoroughly recommend that you try this job yourself. The following steps are a guide to adjusting a bridge with individual saddles. If you have an electronic tuner, plug it directly into the guitar via a jack lead, as this will give a stronger reading than relying on its built-in microphone. The process may seem fiddly, but with practice and patience it becomes easy and rewarding.

Step 1
After tuning up, play the harmonic at the 12th fret of any string. For precise measurement, check the tuning using an electronic tuner.

Step 2
Now compare this harmonic with the fretted note at fret 12. Use just enough pressure for the string to ring true. Keep playing both, one after the other, and listen carefully for any discrepancy between the two. If the two notes sound identical, the string already has perfect intonation.

Step 3
If the fretted note is sharper than the harmonic, it means that the string length is too short. Using the correct type and size of screwdriver, turn the screw that adjusts the saddle's lengthways position (usually found at the rear of the bridge) in a clockwise direction. This will draw the saddle backwards, creating a greater length of string when fretted. Start off with half turns, and repeat this process, from Step 1 (but without tuning up again), until the notes are identical.

If the fretted note is flatter than the harmonic, it means that the string length is too long, and so the opposite procedure applies – screw anti-clockwise to shorten the string length.
Caution: attempting this with the wrong type or size of screwdriver can wreck your bridge!

Step 4
Repeat this process with each string. Using the harmonics and fretted notes at the 19th fret can make the process easier, because at such a high position on the neck any difference is more acute and therefore easier to detect.

A final point
Moving the position of the saddles will slightly affect the height of individual strings by altering the angle at which they pass over the saddles. As a precaution, once you've checked the intonation of every string, you might want to adjust each saddle's height marginally, then re-check the intonation.

MAGNETS, COILS AND POLES

Examining the two basic types of pick-up – single and twin coil.

The actual date when the first pick-up was made is debatable, but a man named Lloyd Loar (under the auspices of the Gibson factory) experimented with pick-ups in the early 1920s. The first guitar to be mass manufactured with a fitted pick-up was Gibson's ES 150, in 1935, which had a fin-shaped pole in the middle of its pick-up. Although this original was far cruder than current pick-ups, the working principle behind it has remained essentially the same.

The basic design

At the core of a pick-up is a magnet, usually made of either a metal called alnico (an alloy of aluminium, nickel and cobalt) or a ceramic (iron and rare earth materials formed into bars under intense pressure and heat). An exceptionally fine copper wire (approximately the same thickness as one human hair) is wrapped around the magnet several thousand times – hence the name 'coil'. Both ends of the copper wire are attached to the guitar's output socket. The wire coils are usually sealed with wax or resin, partially to prevent microphonic feedback caused by the amplification of acoustic sound, which can result in a high-pitched whistling.

The magnet generates a magnetic field around itself, called the flux field, through which the strings pass. Any

A representation of the flux field generated by a pick-up – in this case, a classic PAF Humbucker on a Gibson Les Paul.

vibration in the string moves some of the magnetic lines of force that make up the field. These movements in the field create tiny electrical pulses in the coil. The

pitch of any string is the number of times it vibrates; for example, the A string vibrates at 440 cycles per second, or Herz, which is the reference point for concert pitch on electronic tuners. The coil picks up the same number of vibrations, giving the correct note. The same string struck gently will move less than when it is struck strongly, and so will generate less signal, albeit at an identical frequency.

The stronger the magnet, and the more windings around the coil, the greater the output of the pick-up. However, if a magnet's field is too strong, it can end up restraining the very vibrations it is designed to convert. This undesirable effect is called 'choking'. The type of magnet and the proximity of the coils to the magnets also affect a pick-up's output tone and volume.

Single coil pick-ups

In place of the old bar magnet design, Leo Fender used six individual cylindrical magnets – called pole pieces. These can be altered in height to ensure that each string is detected equally by the pick-up. The coil is wrapped around the pole pieces an amazing 7,600 times. This produces the bright, trebly sound synonymous with Fender guitars. The drawback of this basic version is its susceptibility to picking up interference, or hum, from other electrical sources – for example, a nearby amplifier.

A Fender Telecaster's bridge position single coil pick-up. The six pole pieces are clearly visible.

Twin coil pick-ups – the Humbucker

An engineer at the Gibson guitar factory, the gloriously named Seth Lover, invented the first double coil in 1955. It was specifically designed to remove – or 'buck' in American slang – the interference to which single coil pick-ups were so susceptible (hence the name, 'Humbucker'). It does this by having two coils that are out of phase with each other, i.e. connected in the opposite direction. Any interference is sent by one coil as a positive signal and by the other as a negative signal, and so the two cancel each other out. To ensure that the current generated by the ringing strings is not cancelled out as well, the pole pieces in both coils are attached to opposite poles of the same magnet below, giving them opposite polarities. As a result, the signal produced is actually double that of a single coil. This is why Humbuckers have a fatter sound than single coil pick-ups. The higher level of output also drives amplifier valves harder at the initial stage, adding a characteristic warmth that can distort easily with plenty of sustain. The Humbucker loses some of the bright treble of single coils, but adds more low and mid-range frequencies.

Pick-up height

Pick-ups are usually adjustable for height and angle via screws on the pick-up housing. Broadly speaking, the closer the pick-up is to the string, the louder the output, but being too close can result in the 'choking' described above. The angle determines whether the treble or bass strings will dominate the guitar's sound. Individual pole heights are often adjustable on a single coil pick-up or on one of a double's coils – the height can be adjusted to fine tune the string-to-string output.

A word of warning – careless adjustment with a screwdriver can lead to pick-up fatalities!

Active pick-ups

Active circuitry on a guitar means that there is some level of pre-amplification occurring within the guitar. On standard, passive pick-ups, the signal is limited by the volume and tone controls. It's only when both volume and tone controls are turned right up that the full output of the pick-up is allowed through. Active circuitry for pick-ups (often requiring a separate power source) boosts the pick-ups' signal. Most active tone controls have a central indent position that represents the neutral output. Moving either side of this amplifies particular frequencies. Along with active pick-ups, improved wiring systems and circuitry have led to sophisticated single coil pick-ups, such as the Lace-Sensor pick-ups fitted to many recent Fender models, which manage to eliminate hum without loss of clarity.

Phase switching

If two pick-ups selected together are in phase, the signal is increased. When two pick-ups are out of phase, they partially cancel out each other's signal in the same way that Humbuckers cancel out hum, which leads to a thinner, sharper sound that some players like to use. Many double or single coil guitars have an out-of-phase switch or selector switch position.

Custom pick-ups

There are a wide range of custom pick-ups available to create every shade of tone, attack and volume. Changing the pick-ups is one of the most common customizations of an electric guitar. Di Marzio and Seymour Duncan are two manufacturers who specialize in this field – the latter's pick-ups often feature on manufacturers' deluxe versions of their standard instruments. You can choose

This Strat is fitted with Seymour Duncan pick-ups.

from Humbuckers with a 'vintage' tone or screaming shred metal attack, to single coils with active circuitry or retro styling. Another innovation is the 'stacked pick-up', with one coil on top of another, which combines the tonality of a single coil pick-up with the hum-reducing abilities of a double.

Jonny Greenwood's Telecaster has a double coil pick-up near the bridge and a standard issue single coil further up the neck.

SLIDING AROUND

The evolution of slides, from makeshift Mississippi bottlenecks and knife blades to the wide range of modern tubing now available.

When W.C. Handy, the composer of many classic jazz-Blues songs, was startled at a railway station in Mississippi in 1903 by the sound of a guitarist using a knife as a slide, he described it as 'the weirdest music I have ever heard in my life'. A slide can be used to create effects that just aren't possible with conventional techniques, such as fluid *glissandos* (literally 'sliding' notes), voice-like cries, notes found in between frets and an eerie, shimmering vibrato.

Some of the most compelling Blues music has been played with a slide. The many influential Bluesmen to have used slide include Robert Johnson, Eddie 'Son' House, Tampa Red, Muddy Waters, Elmore James, Blind Willie Johnson and Bukka White. This dramatic style has had an enormous influence on rock music, from The Rolling Stones and Captain Beefheart to acclaimed new acts such as Gomez. Other slide proponents are Ry Cooder (one of the most refined slide stylists) and Rick McCollum of soulful American grunge band Afghan Whigs. McCollum's searing slide is reminiscent of Duane Allman, a 'Seventies slide hero famous for his contribution to Derek And The Dominoes' *Layla*.

Origins and influence

The simple idea of using a hard, smooth object on the strings with the left hand, instead of fretting them, has murky origins and might have been the result of several different influences. Some suggest that it was an offshoot of the Hawaiian style of playing, in which the guitar is tuned to an open chord (hence 'Hawaiian tuning'), placed flat on the lap and then fretted with a smooth rod or bar. This style was invented at the end of the 19th century and grew in popularity in the USA (especially in the South) from 1915 onwards. It was incorporated into country music with the development of lap steel and pedal steel guitars. Blues slide guitar, however, was first played by

Bluesmen from the Mississippi delta area, and the use of 'blue' notes suggests a link with the African music that permeated through generations of slaves.

Slide guitar has now become a standard part of rock music, used to create basic and thrilling riffs or haunting atmospherics. It has also been adopted by Indian classical musicians; Debashish Bhattacharya is a fine exponent of Hindustani slide guitar.

Bottleneck blues

An enormous variety of small, hard objects has been used as slides. Initially, the blunt edge of a knife blade was used by players who sat the guitar flat on their lap. When slide was incorporated into upright playing, hollow tubes were used which could fit onto a left-hand finger. Spark plug sockets, cigar tubes and medicine bottles were all turned to this purpose, but the most common form of slide was a cheap and readily available device – the straight neck of a glass bottle (hence the name). The neck was cut or broken off from the bottle, and the cut ground down until smooth. Some players still use this device today – and Mateus rosé bottlenecks are a popular choice.

Authentic 'medicine bottle'-style bottlenecks.

Modern options

There is now a range of slides available for every taste. The three basic types are glass (usually Pyrex for added durability), metal (steel or brass) and ceramic or porcelain. Broadly speaking, metal slides are louder than glass ones, and many players prefer the smooth, resonant tone of the latter, especially on acoustic guitars. Chromed steel slides give the brightest tone of all and are particularly suitable for use with electrics. Ceramic, a later addition to the slide family, produces a rich, gentle tone, while the density of porcelain gives a bright sound.

Muddy Waters – pictured here using a steel slide on his 4th finger – is one of the most influential electric slide Blues players.

produces a rich, gentle tone, while the density of porcelain gives a bright sound.

Slides come in different widths (to fit different fingers) and various lengths. Full-length slides cover all the strings at once, while short slides cover individual strings. A full-length slide limits left hand flexibility, so tiny slides are now available which cover only one section of the 4th finger, allowing a player to add slide parts and still fret as normal. The weight of a slide is also important, both for comfort and tone.

A selection of glass, chromed steel and brass slides from Jim Dunlop.

Slide works best on guitars with a high action, and this is particularly the case with electrics. 'Pro' slide players often have a guitar set up especially for this purpose, with a higher action than might be comfortable for fretting normally. Heavier gauge strings give a louder, clearer response to a slide, and these also suit the low open tunings deployed by bottleneck players.

Floating fret

The hard, shiny surface of a slide, or bottleneck, acts as a kind of continuous 'floating fret' because the resonating length of a string begins at the precise point at which it is touched by the slide. As a consequence, a slide has to be held directly over any relevant fret, rather than in the normal finger fretting position. For accurate pitch across chords, it should be held absolutely perpendicular to the neck. As a 'floating fret', a slide makes 'blue' notes, equivalent to quarter-note bends, easy to play, as it can glide between fret positions.

Brass slides tapered with a flare – designed to amplify left hand vibrato.

is only practical when playing slide figures and no normal fingerings.

Slide tunings

Slide playing is particularly effective in any of the open tunings to be examined in pages 96-97. These allow you to play a full, shimmering chord just by placing the slide across all the strings at any fret. The 3rd, 5th, 7th and 12th fret positions provide useful chords for a Blues sequence in any open tuning. You *can* play with a slide in standard tuning but because placing the slide across all the strings doesn't produce a usable chord, this requires a good right hand technique to damp unwanted strings. Generally speaking, slide playing produces great results when combined with a fingerpicking technique, and the ability to damp some strings and pluck others is a real asset.

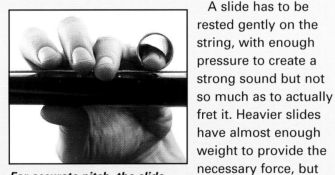

For accurate pitch, the slide must be held directly over the actual fret.

A slide has to be rested gently on the string, with enough pressure to create a strong sound but not so much as to actually fret it. Heavier slides have almost enough weight to provide the necessary force, but the skill of the player remains crucial.

Special techniques

Another technique that is an essential ingredient of slide playing is vibrato, produced by rapid side-to-side movement of the slide (the larger a slide's diameter, the more this movement is exaggerated). This creates notes or chords with oscillating pitch – the eerie, shimmering effect that is the hallmark of slide playing. When combined with the slide equivalent of a hammer-on, delicate pressure and vibrato with a slide can produce notes that ring out without having to be played by the right hand.

Finger options

Which finger the slide is worn on is a question of individual style. When playing chords and sequences that involve fretting with the fingers as well as slide parts, wearing the slide on the 4th finger gives the most fretting options. This also leaves the remaining fingers free to damp the strings lightly above the slide, which reduces unwanted string noise. Some players prefer to use the 3rd finger for its extra strength, but wearing a slide on the 1st or 2nd fingers

Rapid side-to-side movement of a slide produces a distinctive vibrato effect.

POTS, SWITCHES AND SOCKETS

An examination of the bits and pieces that make up the circuit of an electric guitar, and how they work together.

There are a few basic components that, with several possible modifications, you will find inside every electric guitar. This article will tell you what these are, explain how they work, and help you to see how they fit together. Some of the components described have numbers next to them – these numbers refer to the circuit diagram on the opposite page.

1. Circuit wire

All the electrical components are linked by wire that is soldered to each connection to make the circuit. The circuit must have no breaks in it: if it does, the result will be silence. The main flow of signal is carried by a wire with an inner core and an outer screen. The core (also known as the 'hot' wire) carries the signal, while the screen is part of the earthing circuit and acts as a shield.

2. Pick-ups

The guitar's pick-ups produce a small fluctuating current. A traditional single coil pick-up will have two connection points – the 'hot', or live, output and the earth output. Humbuckers have up to four possible output connections because of their double coil construction. We looked at pick-ups in depth on pages 66-67.

Tone and volume controls

The rotating tone and volume knobs are the hand controls for small cylinders called potentiometers, or 'pots' for short. Pots are variable resistors: they limit the amount of signal passing through the circuit to an adjustable degree.

The amount of resistance (known as impedance) between the input connection and either of the output connections changes as the centre of the pot is rotated. The resistance rating of both the tone pot and the volume pot affects the tonal quality and output volume, respectively, of your guitar. The potential resistance value of pots is measured in ohms (denoted by the symbol Ω). The two common pot ratings are 250K and 500K (K = 1,000 ohms). Pots with a higher ohm value give a more subtle volume or tone change.

3. Volume pot

When a volume pot is turned fully off, the resistance between its input and output connections is at the maximum level, while the resistance between its input and the earth output is at the minimum. The signal is now sent to earth and not to the output, so the output seems to have disappeared. In other

words, the pick-ups are still producing a signal but it's being dumped rather than being sent to the amp.

4. Tone pot

The tone pot works in a similar way to the volume pot. It actually acts as a 'treble cut'. This means it can only *reduce* the amount of treble in the signal, so having the tone fully 'up' is simply allowing all the treble through. It does this by sending the signal through a capacitor.

5. Capacitor

Capacitors are small, durable components that act as filters, in this case filtering out treble frequencies. They have very low resistance values measured in microfarads (a millionth of a farad). The basic law is as follows: the lower the value of the capacitor, the greater the cut in treble. The capacitor sets a frequency level below which the tone control pot has no effect but above which the tone control pot can increase the proportion of high frequencies that it sends to earth, in effect cutting these frequencies. Some players like to experiment with the tonal range of their guitar by replacing existing capacitors with ones of different lower or higher values.

6. Jack socket

The jack socket acts as the 'end' of the circuit, connecting the guitar to the amp. The signal arrives here having passed through the tone and volume pots. The socket must be connected to both the earth screen and the inner, live wire.

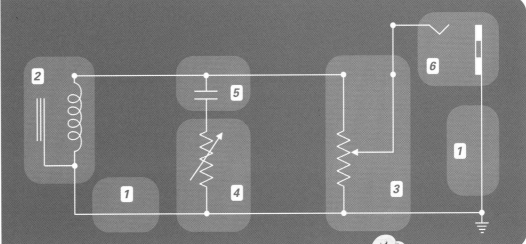

Diagram of a simple, single coil pick-up electric guitar circuit with the components numbered. Use the numbers on the diagram to refer to the numbered headings in the text. A multiple pick-up set-up simply repeats this circuit with the addition of a selector switch between the tone and volume controls and the output socket.

Switches (not shown in circuit)

A pick-up selector switch is basically a junction box that closes and opens connections to different pick-ups.

Extra components

'Coil taps' are sometimes fitted to Humbucker pick-ups. They work as another level of switching by cutting out one of the pick-up's magnets from the circuit. Additional capacitors are sometimes fitted to the volume pots to improve treble output at lower volumes. Active circuitry, which boosts frequencies rather than cuts them, uses a power supply to boost the signal.

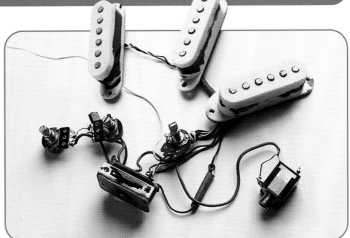

The 'guts' of a Strat-type copy, showing the basic layout of the components. On a Strat-type body, the front panel must be removed to access the circuit after removing the strings. On Gibson-type guitars, the controls are accessible via a panel on the back of the body. DO NOT remove the circuit from a guitar unless you really need to. It necessarily results in broken connections, since the jack socket's connection, and possibly others, have to be broken to be removed.

Earthing

The current generated within a circuit needs to be earthed, or in US terms 'grounded'. Correctly earthing a guitar minimizes hum and makes playing safer. The screen of the main wire should be soldered to the casing of both pots, and all 'earths' should terminate in a single point, because multiple earthing points create hum. Double coil Humbucker pick-ups can be totally grounded within the circuit, but single coil pick-ups are often earthed to the bridge. Unfortunately, this is also common on cheaper double coil guitars. In a set-up such as this, if the earthing should fail on an amplifier, the current will still flow to earth – but through the guitarist, who is now acting as the earth shield! To avoid potential mishaps, putting a circuit-breaker between you and your amp is a sensible safety precaution. Knobs made of a non-conductive material, such as plastic, also increase safety and reduce hum.

Shielding

Shielding, the outer core of circuitry wire, is designed to pick up electrical interference or hum and send it to earth. Pick-ups can be shielded with covers made of a metal or foil that is conductive but that lacks magnetic properties, such as aluminium, copper, brass, gold or silver. It's best if the controls and the output jack are also shielded in this way. Fender paint the inner cavities of their recent models with a carbon-rich conductive paint, an economic form of shielding that reduces hum and makes the guitar even safer to play.

SPEAKER STACKS AND FOLDBACK

The world of live sound equipment explained from a player's perspective.

PAs evolved from public address systems that were designed to carry a voice from a microphone to small speakers via an amplifier. In the early 'Sixties, the popularity of rock'n'roll and its ever-increasing audiences soon overtook the limited technology of old-fashioned vocal systems. The Beatles' famous gig at New York's Shea Stadium in 1963 is a case in point – the audience entirely drowned out the band, so the lads started singing nonsense in the knowledge that the woefully inadequate PA made them inaudible.

Later in the 'Sixties, power trios, such as Cream and The Jimi Hendrix Experience, toured with their own relatively powerful PAs, but these were still primarily intended to amplify only the acoustic sounds (vocals and drums). Guitarists had to make do with the volume provided by vast stacks of speaker cabinets or combos.

The concept of 'sound reinforcement' evolved in the 'Seventies. Miking and direct injection (DI) of every sound source allowed undistorted sound at high volume levels, thanks to powerful amplifiers and speakers designed to project specific frequencies. This helped solve many problems. For example, combo guitar amps project sound only a very small distance, but when miked up and fed through a PA, the sound can fill a vast arena.

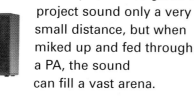

The speakers of a small PA are often mounted on stands to help project the sound.

Vocal PAs and mixer amps

These set-ups are ideal for gigs in intimate venues. Vocal PAs are essentially designed for amplifying the vocals of a singer and any other instruments that might need the help. Acoustic guitars with built-in pick-ups can be plugged straight into them, or miked-up in the more traditional way through a PA such as this without too much trouble. Amplifiers for small PAs, which are also common in rehearsal rooms, are usually mixer-style amps.

A Kustom 60 watt mixer amp, ideal for small venues.

These have separate channels with individual gain and tone controls, which allow you to amplify several different signals at once. A master volume control determines the overall output of the amplifier.

Getting the best from a small PA

- The speakers of a small PA can take some high-pressure signals (such as a bass drum) individually, but they will struggle to project several signals (such as vocals, guitar and drums) clearly at the same time.
- When plugging an acoustic guitar straight into a mixer amp, keep the initial level of gain low to avoid unwanted feedback and distortion.
- Built-in transducers in acoustic guitars tend towards the bright side, so go easy on the treble.

You are likely to come across your first proper PA, or 'rig', in medium-sized venues, such as pubs and clubs. It will most probably have the following basic components.

Monitors, or foldback speakers

These speakers face backwards so that the performers can hear what they and the other band members are playing. What and how much is heard in these monitors depends on the mix. This is either controlled from the main mixing desk or, in larger venues, from a separate, dedicated desk. Monitors come in all shapes and sizes, but the most common, placed near the players' feet, are 'wedges', so called because of their shape.

A high-quality wedge monitor made by HK Audio.

Mikes and DI boxes

Drums, guitar combos and vocals all tend to be miked. Guitar amps are usually 'close miked' with a unidirectional microphone, which is pointed at the edge of the speaker. (We will deal with mikes and their positioning later.) Acoustic and bass guitars can be sent to the mixing desk via a DI box, which puts the control of their sound in the hands of the engineer.

A standard DI box.

Multicore

The many signals from all the on-stage microphones and DIs are sent to the mixing desk via a neat bundle of cables called the multicore.

A multicore cable and connection box.

Mixing desk

Before being sent to the amplifier, all signals pass through a mixing desk, which is usually situated in the optimum listening position in front of the speakers. The desk is made up of several identical 'channels'. Each one has controls for the initial gain level of each signal, some kind of EQ (tone control) adjustment, a fader to adjust the individual volume of each channel in the overall sound, and auxiliary channels that can send the signal to effects units, such as reverb. The effects units and EQs, or 'outboard gear', are usually stacked to one side of the mixing desk, within easy reach of the engineer. As well as boosting any frequency, the EQ can be used to 'tweak out' particular frequencies that might be causing feedback. (We will look at the workings of a mixing desk in greater detail on pages 76-77.)

Power amplifiers and speakers

These range from around 100 watts or more for small PAs up to several thousands of watts for more powerful systems. One thousand watts is a kilowatt, often referred to as a 'K'. Amps of a moderate output can be linked up to 'slave' amplifiers (so called because they do the hard work), which re-amplify the initial signal to provide even more volume. Large systems can use several slave amplifiers, driven from the mixing desk, through an active crossover unit, which divides the amplified signal into various frequency bands. These, in turn, are sent to their own dedicated speakers. The specialized speakers that handle the bass

frequencies are referred to as bass bins, cabs or bottoms. The sound generated by all the speakers that point towards the audience is referred to as the 'front of house' sound.

The SRA 600 power amplifier made by Roland.

Backline

This is jargon for all on-stage guitar, bass or keyboard amps. Much of the art of good live mixing in a medium-sized venue is ensuring that the sound coming from the PA complements the sound that is already being produced by the backline.

Soundcheck suggestions

- Check all leads and equipment before setting off to the gig. Tuning up before the soundcheck saves time.
- Take the time to let the sound engineer know exactly what your line-up requires – how many DI boxes, vocal mikes, etc., as well as what you want to hear in your monitors.
- Be prepared to turn down your amp if the engineer asks you to, as this will give him more control over its level in the mix.

The mixing desk of the PA of the Bull and Gate, a well-equipped pub venue in North London that caters for new and original acts. The rack of equipment to the right of the desk is the 'outboard gear' – effects units, compressors, noise gates and EQs.

STUCK INTO MIDI WITH YOU

Back to the future with analogue synth-axes and digital pick-ups.

The first production synthesizer was manufactured by the Moog company in 1964. The seemingly limitless varieties of sounds produced by synths since then revolutionized the way music could be made, and there was talk of synths permanently replacing guitars as a band's lead instrument. Although this didn't happen, synthesizer and guitar technology did come together, offering new and exciting hybrids.

Guitar trigger

Although synths are usually thought of as a form of keyboard, this doesn't have to be the case. The keyboard is simply a convenient way of triggering the tones generated by the synthesizer unit. In practice, this 'trigger' can take many shapes or forms – including that of a guitar.

This extraordinary-looking Spanish guitar has MIDI pads fitted across its soundboard, which enable the player to trigger a variety of percussion sounds and synth effects.

Roland guitar synths

Early guitar synths were essentially control units for specially built analogue synthesizers. However, they were very limited in expression and took great patience to master. The Roland company were pioneers of guitar-synth technology in the 'Seventies, and the first such instrument commercially available was the Roland GS-500. This was a Les Paul-shaped guitar synth controller, joined via a cable the size of a garden hose to a large analogue synth unit, the GS-500.

Andy Summers of The Police and Jimmy Page of Led Zeppelin were both keen users of Roland guitar synths in the 'Eighties – Summers used them on *Synchronicity*, while Page did so on *In Through The Out Door*. One 'Eighties Roland model, the G-707, is remembered as much for its ray-gun looks as for its usability. It was sold with the GR-700 analogue synthesizer that came in the form of a huge pedalboard with enough memory for 64 different 'patches', or configurations of sound and channel assignment.

MIDI technology

Developed by the Sequential Circuits company in 1981, MIDI revolutionized the music industry. MIDI – short for Musical Instrument Digital Interface – is a system enabling digital instruments and units to 'talk' to each other, via five-pin 'DIN' cable connections. This allowed sequencers to be used to trigger sounds on other MIDI instruments. The MIDI system also meant that guitars, if fitted with MIDI pick-ups, could be used to play MIDI synthesizers. (NB: Many digital multiple-effects units have a MIDI 'In', 'Through' and 'Out' facility. This useful addition allows changes in the settings of effects units to be triggered by another piece of equipment. This is not the same as playing a MIDI guitar synth.)

MIDI pick-ups

To play a synthesizer using a guitar as the controller, or trigger, the physical vibration and movement of the strings have to be 'translated' into signals that will inform the synthesizer about the pitch qualities, volume, and 'envelope' information (the attack, sustain and decay of a note) it should generate in response. The first stage of this process occurs at the pick-up, which has to be a specialized MIDI one.

One current industry-standard MIDI pick-up is the Roland GK-2 that evolved from the 'hex' pick-up found on Roland's early guitar synths. It can be fitted to any guitar and is usually mounted on the body below the bridge. GK-2 pick-ups are available separately, but many guitars, including the American Standard

The angular G-707 Roland guitar synth, with a 'stabilizer bar' linking the headstock to the body. Note the 'hex' pick-up near the bridge.

The slim pick-up can be fitted between the lead pick-up and bridge.

Roland's GK-2A MIDI pick-up.

Output can be switched between MIDI synth signal, the 'natural' guitar signal, or a mix of the two.

GR Strat and Ovation 'Roland-ready' electro-acoustic guitars, come with them already installed.

Takamine manufacture a MIDI-ready classical guitar with a 'Shadow' pick-up fitted. Also, John Birch make a series of custom guitars that come equipped with their own brand of MIDI pick-up.

Pitch-to-signal converters

The signal from the MIDI pick-up has to be sent through a MIDI pitch-to-signal converter unit. These converters are often combined with synths in one unit, as is the case with the majority of Roland's GR modules and John Birch's M3 unit. Once converted, the signal can be used to play any MIDI synthesizer.

The basic elements of a MIDI set-up appear in many different configurations. Starr Labs make the Ztar, an extraordinary-looking 'space-age' MIDI guitar, which has a built-in pitch-to-MIDI converter, along with an optional synthesizer board attachment.

Above: a John Birch model with their 'Full-Range' MIDI pick-ups ready fitted.

Right: The GR-30, a guitar synth module in the player-friendly form of a foot-switchable unit.

Don't forget your amps

The last stage of the MIDI guitar process is the amplifier. Although the guitar's actual sound can be blended in with the synth sound, the tones being produced by a MIDI guitar set-up are generated by the synth – the guitar simply acts as the trigger. As a result, the best amplified sound is achieved with a keyboard amp, or a small PA amp. Synthesizers tend to have stereo output, so stereo amplifiers will produce the most impressive results.

PC guitar

In the early days of MIDI, the price of specialized MIDI gear was relatively prohibitive, but recently it has become more affordable in budget versions. With a MIDI pick-up, a pitch-to-signal converter and the right software, it is now possible to trigger and control sequencing and synthesizer programs on a PC with your guitar.

Problems and difficulties

Many of the limitations and drawbacks of early guitar synths were due to their inability to process all the information about string vibration and pitch. The G-707, for example, couldn't send information about bending notes – the notes would simply be on or off, as if triggered by a keyboard. The result, of course, sounded stilted in comparison with normal guitar playing. Improvements in technology, however, have made pitch-bend conversion a standard and affordable feature.

Sensitivity

Setting up a MIDI guitar system is a painstaking process. The heights of the poles of a MIDI pick-up have to be fine-tuned to give a consistent signal, while at the other end, the synthesizer's response has to be carefully adjusted to provide a workable set-up. Each guitar string can be assigned a different sound on the synthesizer, and each of those sounds given different response parameters.

Any note played on the guitar will make the synthesizer generate one in turn, so accidental notes will register and therefore trigger unwanted synth sounds. As a result, MIDI guitar playing requires fastidiously accurate technique.

PLAY AND RECORD

Getting guitar onto tape, from the home set-up to the professional studio.

First launched 20 years ago by Tascam, the multi-track 'portastudio' (originally a brand name but now used as a generic term) remains the cheapest and most popular way of recording at home. Yamaha and Fostex are also reputable makes. With all the brands, the cost of multi-tracks varies according to their specifications and facilities. Many players treat their portable multi-track as an indispensable sketch pad, good for recording any ideas that come to mind, but with a little care the results can be good enough to release. Much of Gomez's award-winning début album was recorded on a home multi-track set-up before being remixed in a studio.

Cassettes and running speed
Although some multi-tracks can cope with metal cassettes, the majority give the best results with the chrome (position II) variety. TDK's SA-X is one of the best cassettes of this type. Whereas a stereo cassette deck plays and records on only two tracks (one for each stereo channel) on one half of the cassette tape's width, a four-track recorder uses the whole width of the tape to record four tracks.

Tape speed both on multi-track and reel-to-reel machines is measured in ips, or inches per second. The higher the running speed of a machine, the better the tonal quality of its recording and playback because more tape is used to record the signal. For this reason, the more elaborate multi-tracks can run at double speed. Eight-track machines halve the width of tape used for each track to double the number of tracks they can record. To compensate for the resulting loss of quality, eight-track cassette decks always run at double speed.

Microphones
A couple of reasonable microphones, along with a stand for positioning them, are an essential part of a home recording set-up. For recording guitar, a good quality, unidirectional mike – such as a Sure SM57 – will suffice. (A unidirectional mike records sound from only one direction.) Tandy/Radioshack make a PZM (Pressure Zone Microphone), which is an excellent and very inexpensive ambient mike. It can record high-volume levels with great clarity, capturing the ambient sound of a room, making it very useful for recording full band rehearsals.

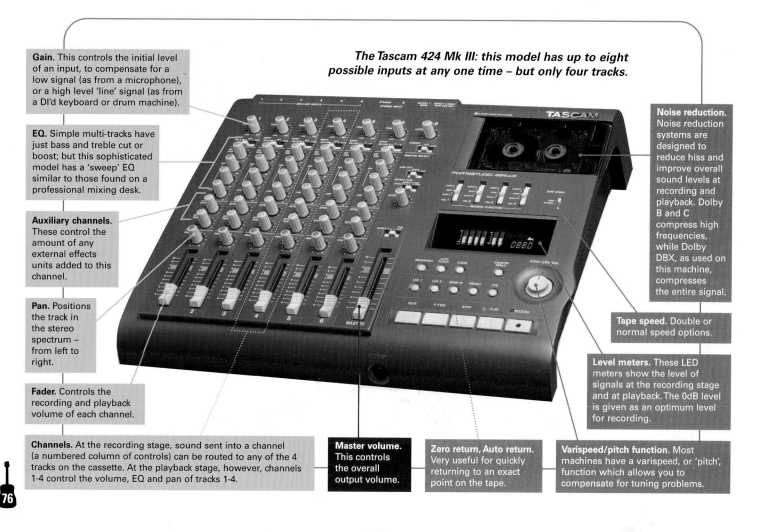

The Tascam 424 Mk III: this model has up to eight possible inputs at any one time – but only four tracks.

Gain. This controls the initial level of an input, to compensate for a low signal (as from a microphone), or a high level 'line' signal (as from a DI'd keyboard or drum machine).

EQ. Simple multi-tracks have just bass and treble cut or boost; but this sophisticated model has a 'sweep' EQ similar to those found on a professional mixing desk.

Auxiliary channels. These control the amount of any external effects units added to this channel.

Pan. Positions the track in the stereo spectrum – from left to right.

Fader. Controls the recording and playback volume of each channel.

Noise reduction. Noise reduction systems are designed to reduce hiss and improve overall sound levels at recording and playback. Dolby B and C compress high frequencies, while Dolby DBX, as used on this machine, compresses the entire signal.

Tape speed. Double or normal speed options.

Level meters. These LED meters show the level of signals at the recording stage and at playback. The 0dB level is given as an optimum level for recording.

Channels. At the recording stage, sound sent into a channel (a numbered column of controls) can be routed to any of the 4 tracks on the cassette. At the playback stage, however, channels 1-4 control the volume, EQ and pan of tracks 1-4.

Master volume. This controls the overall output volume.

Zero return, Auto return. Very useful for quickly returning to an exact point on the tape.

Varispeed/pitch function. Most machines have a varispeed, or 'pitch', function which allows you to compensate for tuning problems.

RECORDING TIPS AND TECHNIQUES

Signal levels

To get the best quality signal for playback with the minimum of tape noise, you should aim to record a signal at the optimum level. Experiment to see how far you can push a signal 'into the red' at the recording stage before it overloads and distorts, which might be slightly above the 0dB (zero decibels) level on the meter.

Miking up

Amplifiers can be miked up with a unidirectional microphone. Experiment with the effects that different mike positions have on the sound. The standard approach is to point the mike at the edge of the speaker cone, but miking some distance away gives
a more open-sounding result. Acoustic guitars are harder to mike up; you could try close-miking near the soundhole, although acoustics with built-in pick-ups can also be DI'd.

Amp simulators

A short-cut way of recording an electric guitar is to plug the guitar straight into an amp simulator. Amp simulators are digital effects units that mimic the sound of various classic amps in a variety of miking set-ups.

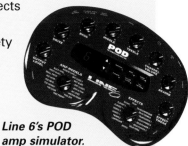

Line 6's POD amp simulator.

Bouncing

Having four tracks doesn't limit you to just four separate takes or instruments. Two tracks can be played back and recorded as one onto another track – a technique called 'bouncing' or 'ping-ponging'. The Beatles used bouncing to create the multi-layered textures of their 1967 *Sgt. Pepper's* album, which was recorded on a humble four-track.

Minidisc multi-tracks

These machines are at the more expensive end of the multi-track market. They function in a similar way to cassette multi-tracks, but instead record digitally onto minidisc, which makes for crisp, high-fidelity recordings.

The professional recording studio

Recording studios have at least two rooms – the playing room, or booth, and the control room. The playing room might have natural, or 'dead', areas (these are acoustically muffled to have the minimum resonance and sound reflection), as well as 'live' areas (which are acoustically bright). Amps are often recorded in the dead areas to give a very pure sound.

The control room contains the mixing desk and the recorder itself – the reel-to-reel machine. Measured by the width of tape that they run, reel-to-reel machines range from quarter-inch, eight-track machines to four-inch, 48-track models. Digital studios record directly onto hard drive. The mixing desk is actually simpler than it looks and is built on a modular basis, of identical vertical strips. Each strip has fader controls for level, EQ and auxiliary effects.

Mastering

Whether you record on a portastudio or at a 48-track professional studio, your music still has to be mastered before it can be listened to or copied. Mastering involves mixing all the tracks into just two (i.e. down to stereo). DAT (digital audio tape) is an industry standard for this process. You can, of course, master home recordings onto a standard cassette deck.

Acoustically 'dead' sound booth, ideal for recording vocals or another isolated sound source.

The 'business end' of the studio, a Tascam one-inch reel-to-reel 24-track recorder.

A Soundtracs mixing desk. The raised back holds the level meter displays for each channel. The mass of red cables on the right of the desk are links to the outboard

Main 'live' area, with enough room to record a whole band, using 'baffles' to improve separation.

These Yamaha NS-10s are standard monitors. The sound from these is compared with a larger set of speakers.

View of the mixing desk at Scarlet Studios, a 24-track studio situated in North London.

TIMING AND NOTE VALUES

An in-depth look at rhythm and how this essential component of music is conveyed throughout Guitar Essentials.

Over the following pages, we will be clarifying some of the music theory that has cropped up so far, but which may not have been explained in any great detail. We'll look at rhythm, pitch, notation, scales, arpeggios, key signatures, and chords and their labels.

We begin with timing – a vital element of good guitar playing. It is often the timing of the pieces that is the most difficult part to master. Timing is all about playing your notes or chords on the right beat, knowing how long to let them ring, or how long to rest before moving on to the next note. Proficiency in this area will ensure that your playing is always tight and rhythmical.

Note symbols

On page 14, we briefly explained the time values of the standard notation symbols that appear above the TAB line. It's worth paying close attention to these symbols because the TAB numbers alone won't show you how long notes or rests are supposed to last. In the box below is a concise recap of these notation symbols.

Bars and bar lines

Notes are divided equally into what are known as bars. These divisions are shown in the TAB below the time values by vertical lines called bar lines. These mark the beginning and end of each bar of music.

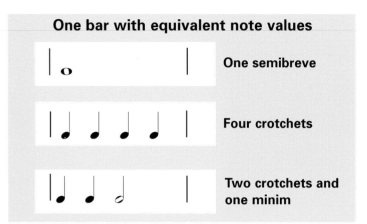

One bar with equivalent note values

One semibreve

Four crotchets

Two crotchets and one minim

Dotted notes

There are times when a slightly longer or shorter note is needed than those discussed so far. A dot after a note achieves this finer grading by increasing the length of a note by another half of its time value.

Note values and their names

Semibreve 	The longest note you'll come across is a semibreve. The Americans call it a whole note	**Crotchet**	This is called a crotchet, or quarter note, and lasts for a count of one beat.

because it takes up a whole bar. Whatever its name, it lasts for a count of four. These counts are referred to as beats.

Quaver

This is called a quaver, or eighth note, and lasts for half a beat.

Minim

This is called a minim, or half note, and lasts for a count of two beats.

Semiquaver

This is called a semi-quaver, or 16th note, and lasts for quarter of a beat.

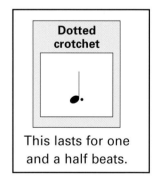

Dotted crotchet

This lasts for one and a half beats.

Time signatures

A new and important concept to understand is that of time signatures, which tell you how many beats there are in a bar, as well as the time value of each of those beats. Time signatures are usually represented in standard notation by two numbers, written as a fraction (e.g. $\frac{4}{4}$). The number below represents the time value of the beats, while the number above shows how many beats there are to each bar.

Examples of time signature

The majority of rock music have a time signature of $\frac{4}{4}$ – which represents a count of four crotchets to a bar. This means that each bar of music has a time value that always adds up to the equivalent of four one-count crotchets, or quarter notes.

In the 8th bar of Metallica's *One*, for example, the riff changes into $\frac{2}{4}$ time, giving a count of two beats per bar (which is half the previous count of $\frac{4}{4}$).

Another example of an irregular time signature is *The Riverboat Song* by Ocean Colour Scene has a time signature of $\frac{6}{8}$, meaning that each bar has the equivalent of six eighth-beat notes.

Rests

The other main group of symbols used in sheet music are rests – the marks that indicate that nothing should be played at all. You need these to show pauses in riffs, or damped silences in between chords, for example. Without them, music would just be a stream of continuous notes. Keith Richards, for one, has always maintained that good guitar playing is as much about what you don't play as what you do – he calls it 'sculpting with silence'. There are rest equivalents for every note value, and rests can be dotted to extend them in exactly the same manner as notes.

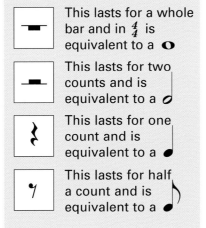

▬	This lasts for a whole bar and in $\frac{4}{4}$ is equivalent to a 𝅝
▬	This lasts for two counts and is equivalent to a 𝅗𝅥
𝄽	This lasts for one count and is equivalent to a 𝅘𝅥
𝄾	This lasts for half a count and is equivalent to a 𝅘𝅥𝅮

Tied notes

A tie, shown as a curved line between two note heads, is used to link notes that are sustained. For example, a note that should be sustained for two whole bars of $\frac{4}{4}$ (which is a count of eight beats) is shown by two tied semibreves, one at the beginning of each bar, although the note is actually struck only once. Linking notes across bar lines is a common use of ties.

You may have noticed that quavers are often joined, or 'beamed', at the top. This is done to group them together, which in turn makes them easier to read. However, if a quaver is played in isolation, off the beat (i.e. it falls between the main counts), it generally won't

be joined to a successive quaver. In any bar that is in $\frac{4}{4}$, all the note and rest symbols have to add up to the value of four counts.

Sample bars

A quick glance through any piece of rock sheet music will reveal how varied the composition of a bar in $\frac{4}{4}$ can be. For example, look at these two bars, which represent the rhythm of the chord strum from *This is a Call* by The Foo Fighters:

The first note, which is a crotchet, falls on the first beat, while the second, which is a quaver, falls on the second beat. Notice that the quavers are beamed together, into two pairs, and that these two pairs are joined by a tie. The tie means that the third strummed chord is left ringing for twice as long as the second. The note in the last bar is left ringing for a whole count of four. The following rests are from the same song:

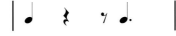

After the first one-count crotchet note, there is a rest for one count. Then a half-count quaver rest is followed by a dotted crotchet, which lasts one and a half counts. Notice that all the note and rest values within the bar add up to a total of four counts.

Try playing the following rhythm, taking care to strike the string only where it is indicated by an arrow.

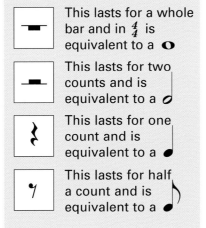

Do you recognise it? It's *The James Bond Theme*. The first quaver note is joined to two semiquavers. These are followed by two beamed half-count notes, the second of which is left ringing (hence the tie) for a further half count. Three half-count quaver notes conclude the rhythm.

NOTES AND CHORDS

We will now focus on chords and notes, starting with 'primary' chords (the set of chords that underlie most sequences). We begin with the primary chords for the key of C major. You don't have to understand all the theory, but the simple sequence we are about to reveal is found in the vast majority of guitar-based music, be it Blues, folk, rock, reggae or pop, and as such it is a milestone in your learning. Throughout these features we refer to popular songs with which you should be familar.

THE MAJOR SCALE, IN C
A look at the construction of a major scale and the notes that make up a major chord.

In this feature, we look at the theory behind a major scale, where to play it and how it works. Over the next pages, we look at other scales in order to develop your musical vocabulary. To start off, we will use the scale of C major, which is the simplest scale because it contains no flats or sharps.

TAB of C major scale

Below is the TAB for a one-octave C major scale using only the notes found in the 1st position – the 1st finger placed at fret 1, the 2nd at fret 2, the 3rd at fret 3 and the 4th at fret 4. The scale is also written above the TAB in standard music notation.

The notes are C, D, E, F, G, A, B and C, ending at C an octave above the starting C. (These follow the *doh re mi fa soh la te doh* pattern that will be familiar to fans of *The Sound of Music*.) The number of steps, or semitones, from one of these notes to the next is very important, as the sequence of steps between notes is what differentiates one type of scale from another. The major scale, for instance, has a different pattern of steps from the minor scale. In tones and semitones, the pattern of the C major scale is C to D (tone), D to E (tone), E to F (semitone), F to G (tone), G to A (tone), A to B (tone) and B to C (semitone). The pattern for the major scale is, therefore, Tone – Tone – Semitone – Tone – Tone – Tone – Semitone (T T S T T T S).

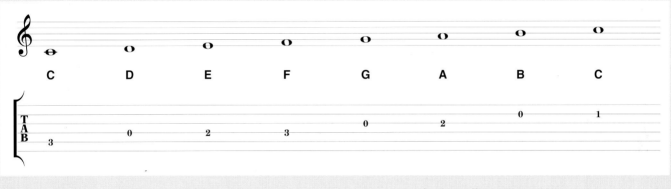

The C major scale written in both TAB and standard notation, using notes that are all found at the first three frets. Notice that in the standard notation, the notes move up in position from a line to a space each time.

TAB of C major scale on the 5th string

Playing the C major scale on one string only, starting at the 3rd fret of the A string, clearly shows the relation of one fret to one semitone. This relates directly to the major scale sequence of T T S T T T S as two frets – two frets – one fret – two frets – two frets – two frets – one fret. This sequence is the same for every note's major scale and can therefore be used as a template to build any major scale. Start with your chosen note, then find the notes that occur at these intervals after it until you arrive back at the original note, one octave higher.

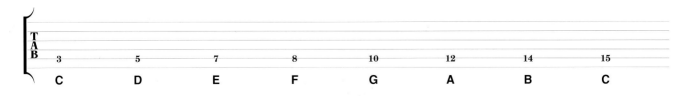

Playing the C major scale on only one string – in this case the 5th string – clearly demonstrates how every fret equals one semitone. It also shows that a note 12 frets up from any given fret is one octave higher.

The C major chord

Take a look at the notes that make up a C chord. (Often the C major chord is simply referred to as the C chord, whereas a minor chord is always specified as being minor.) Fret the chord and play each string one by one, starting at string 5 and working across the strings.

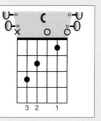

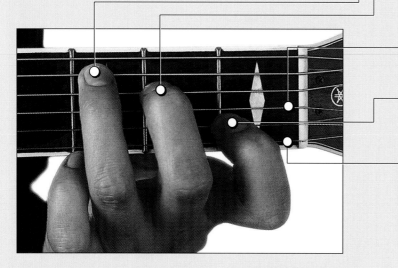

The first note is C. As this is a C chord, it makes sense that the scale starts with a C. This is called the 'root' note because it is the first step in the scale.

Next up is E, which is the 2nd fret on string 4. E is the 3rd note in the C major scale, called the major third.

Then comes the open G string. G is the 5th note in the C major scale.

Fret 1 on the 2nd string provides another C, the 8th note in the major scale, and therefore an octave above the root note.

This is followed by the open 1st string, which is another E. This means that C, E, G, C (an octave above) and E (an octave above) are all played simultaneously to form a C major chord. So the C major chord is actually made up of only three note names – C, E and G, with both E and C being repeated an octave above.

Just as all major scales follow the same step sequence, so every major chord is made up of the 1st, 3rd and 5th steps of that note's major scale. These are often supplemented by the 8th note of the major scale, an octave up from the root note, plus different octaves of the 3rd or 5th notes of the major scale. Try analysing the notes found in the other major chords we have used so far – E, G, D, A – and you'll find that they all follow this pattern.

Notice how the lowest note in every chord has a dominating effect. This is why, even though E is the major third of C and is found elsewhere in the chord, you should avoid playing the bottom open E string because it would bias the sound of the chord towards that note rather than the C. Try playing the open E with the chord to hear the difference.

Above: The C major chord represented in both TAB (left) and standard music notation (right). The notes are stacked vertically because, in a chord, they're all played at once. The lowest note is the root note C, followed by an E and a G, plus another C and E one octave higher. The C chord is an easy one to recognize in standard notation; as the only major chord without flats or sharps, it is represented solely by straightforward note symbols.

Variations within major chords

The notes that are required to form a major chord don't have to occur in the same order or even in the same octave – they just have to be there. The chord can also be played with an open 2nd string, which gives it two Bs – fret 2 on the 5th string and the open 2nd string. B is the 3rd note in the G major scale. They are both correct G major chords, each with a slightly different feel; the one with two D notes is often referred to as a 'full' G chord.

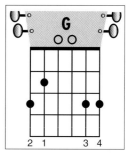

G major chord with string 2 at fret 3.

G major chord with open string 2.

POWER CHORDS

Previously, we explained the sequence of a C major scale and the formation of the major chord. Building on that, we will now examine the power chord.

Power chords, labelled as '5 chords, use only the guitar's lower strings. This concentration upon the bass notes produces the sort of deep, punchy sounds that are perfectly suited to rock music.

A reminder of the major chord

On page 82, we outlined how the major chord must contain notes 1, 3 and 5 from the major scale. Duplicates of one or more of these notes often occur at higher octaves, creating four-, five- or six-string chords. Remind yourself of the C major chord, first featured in Issue 5, and the notes C, E and G that form it.

Removing the 3rd from the major chord

C5, the C power chord, is so called because it is made up of only the root note C plus its 5th, G. Compare it with a C major chord and you will hear that it lacks the major flavour. This is because the 3rd note of the C major scale – the E, which makes it sound major – is absent.

Three-string power chords

The addition of the octave above the root note intensifies a '5 chord without introducing a change of harmony.

Like the template for the C major scale, you can make up a '5 chord for any note by adding the 5th step of its major scale to the root note. Check this with any of the power chords that appear in this issue, and try making up

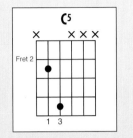

Above: The C5 chord consists of the notes C and G.

Above: The C power chord shown in standard music notation.

Right: The C power chord as it appears in the TAB.

some of your own.

Power chords are a kind of shorthand for full chords. It is the lack of a 3rd and the strength of the perfect 5th that earns the chord the name 'power chord'.

Soon we will take a close look at minor chords, which use a different type of 3rd to colour their sound, and the minor scale from which they are formed.

An in-depth look at C5 using three strings

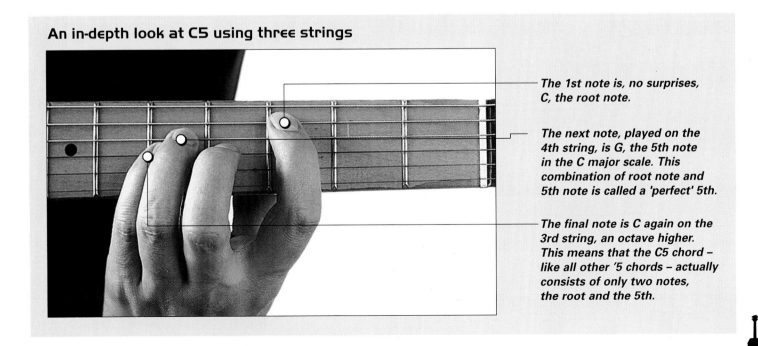

The 1st note is, no surprises, C, the root note.

The next note, played on the 4th string, is G, the 5th note in the C major scale. This combination of root note and 5th note is called a 'perfect' 5th.

The final note is C again on the 3rd string, an octave higher. This means that the C5 chord – like all other '5 chords – actually consists of only two notes, the root and the 5th.

THE MINOR SCALE, IN A

Following on from the look at the major scale, we now examine the notes that make up the A minor chord, and the construction of the minor scale.

Played on their own, or at the beginning of a song, minor chords have a 'sad' effect – as in *The House Of The Rising Sun* by the Animals – but when played in between major chords, they have a different, less melancholic effect. We examine what gives minor chords this distinctive quality.

The A minor chord

Take a look at the notes that make up the A minor chord, first featured back in Issue 1. Fret the chord and play each string one by one, beginning with the open 5th string, which provides the root note A. The note E on the 4th string is the 5th, followed by another A an octave above the original.

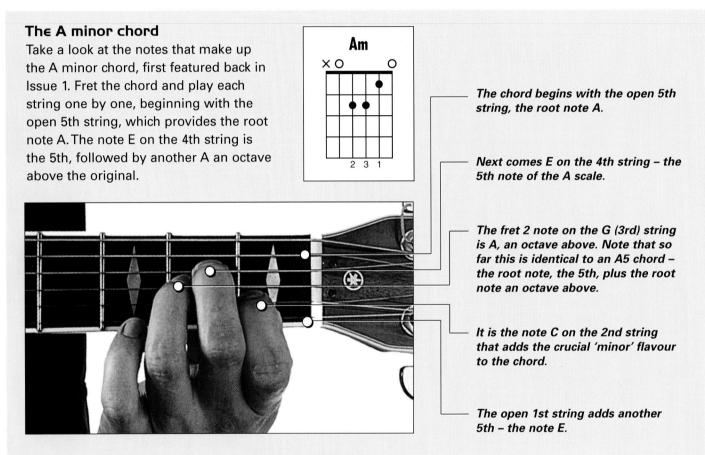

The chord begins with the open 5th string, the root note A.

Next comes E on the 4th string – the 5th note of the A scale.

The fret 2 note on the G (3rd) string is A, an octave above. Note that so far this is identical to an A5 chord – the root note, the 5th, plus the root note an octave above.

It is the note C on the 2nd string that adds the crucial 'minor' flavour to the chord.

The open 1st string adds another 5th – the note E.

So far these notes are the same as for an A5 chord. It's the next note, C, that makes the crucial difference to the sound of the chord. This C is followed by another E an octave above the first one, doubling up the 5th.

Try playing a C chord after an A minor, an easy change to make. The two chords have some of the same fingering in common; fingers 1 and 2 remain in the same place, while finger 3 leaves the G (3rd) string and moves to fret 3 on the A (5th) string to make the root note C. The chords sound related too, as they both have a C and an E in them. It is the C note in the A minor chord that appears to be giving the chord its minor quality – in fact, A minor is referred to as the 'relative' minor of C.

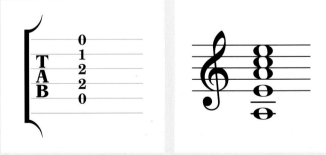

Above: The A minor chord in TAB and notation. Notice that A minor resembles C major (see pages 81-82) in that the 1st, 2nd and 4th string notes are exactly the same, and neither chord contains any sharps or flats.

The A major chord

Now compare the minor chord to A major, played, for example, in *Pretty Vacant* by The Sex Pistols. The only difference between these two chord shapes is the 2nd string note – C# in the major, C in the minor. Play the A major scale (shown below in 1st position), constructed using the major scale pattern of T T S T T T S that was laid out in page 81. It's clear that C# is the 3rd note in the A major scale.

Above: The A major chord features a C sharp – the only difference between it and A minor.

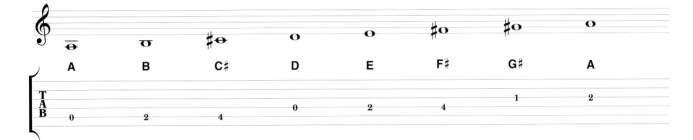

Building the natural minor scale

Minor scales are not as clear-cut as their major counterparts since they exist in three subtly different forms – the natural minor, harmonic minor and melodic minor. For now, we shall focus on the natural minor. Play the following natural minor scale in A, built upon a different sequence of note steps from the major scale. The pattern for any natural minor scale is T S T T S T T. A tone (T) is a distance of two frets from one note to the next, whereas a semitone (S) is a distance of only one fret.

The A natural minor scale in TAB and notation. The intervals between the ascending notes are T S T T S T T.

The minor 3rd

You will recall that your chord shapes use notes 1, 3 and 5 of the scale. Immediately, you can hear and see that notes 1 and 5 (A and E) are the same in both A major and A minor. The crucial difference affects the 3rd note – C# in A major, and C, a fret lower, in A minor. The distance between the 1st and 3rd notes is smaller in A minor, and so it is referred to as a 'minor 3rd'.

Building minor chords

Check out the occurrence of the minor 3rd in all the minor chords studied so far. Compare E major with its minor (right); the removal of your 1st finger from fret 1 of the G (3rd) string clearly shows the semitone difference between the major and minor 3rd.

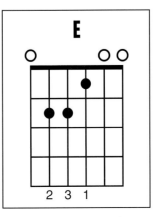

E major chord with the G string at fret 1.

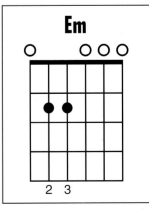

E minor chord with the G string open.

FINGERS AND THUMBS

A look at the other half of guitar playing – right hand finger work – which can turn straightforward chords into dynamic, rhythmic accompaniments.

Fingerpicking

In *Say What You Want* by Texas a distinctive guitar sound is created by a simple right hand picking pattern. This finger style technique can be referred to as 'fingerpicking', and its roots lie in folk, country and western and the Blues. Fingerpicking is based around independent movement of the right hand thumb and fingers. The thumb tends to play a rhythmic bass line, with notes falling on the main beats of the bar, while the fingers pick out the melody or upper strings. This style can be heard in the simple but effective patterns of folk heroes, such as Woody Guthrie and Bob Dylan.

Blues style

The fingerpicking technique lies at the heart of the folk Blues guitar played by Blues heroes, such as Blind Lemon Jefferson, Bukka White and the great Leadbelly. The insistent bass notes provide a driving beat, the 'boogie' that John Lee Hooker loves so dearly.

Picking variations

There are many refinements and variations within fingerpicking, including partial damping of bass notes with the heel of the right hand, and the 'claw hammer' style, as used by The Reverend Gary Davis. This is so called because only the index and middle finger are used to 'claw' upstrokes, while the thumb picks out the bass. The alternating bass notes and finger patterns can be set against deft left hand chord work to create bewitching sequences of notes, rich in harmonic interplay. Used in conjunction with open tunings, the talent of some British folk guitarists, such as Richard Thompson, Adrian Legge, John Martyn and Nick Drake, has elevated folk fingerpicking to the level of a fine art.

A muffled-up John Martyn picks at his acoustic.

Flatpicking

Playing bass notes and then chords with a plectrum, and picking out the lower strings as a deliberate part of the strum pattern, is called 'flatpicking'. This style is prevalent in country music – the 'dum-chinga-dum' strum typifies the songs of Johnny Cash. Flatpicking can be combined with fingerpicking – the plectrum is held between the thumb and forefinger to play the bass notes, while the remaining fingers pluck the top strings. Many great players, such as Scotty Moore, Eric Clapton and Richard Thompson favour this method for the sheer versatility it allows.

Thumbpicks and fingerpicks

For many players, the fingertips produce an adequate sound. Some grow their fingernails to achieve a stronger tone, while others prefer the strident, clear sound (on a steel string) of thumb- and/or fingerpicks made of plastic or metal.

Classical (Spanish) and Latin American finger styles

Classical guitarists would never consider using anything other than the right hand fingers. Every string is played in a flexible, ever-changing way and rarely with a fixed, repeated picking pattern. Instead, the fingers play the instrument as a fluid whole, combining both melody and accompaniment, with many variations in rhythm and pattern from bar to bar, using all four fingers. Students of classical guitar begin to develop this degree of right hand skill from the outset of their playing, and this is one of the many reasons why classically trained players tend to be among the most technically proficient.

Flamenco playing

Flamenco players go one step further in terms of their right hand – they acquire the skill of using each individual finger to play rapid alternate strokes. Flamenco players also hit the soundboard percussively with the right hand, a technique called *golpe*.

Electric picking

At one time, some form of fingerpicking was the only style available to guitar players. However, as amplification allowed players to solo with single-note lines, without fear of being drowned out, so electric players tended to rely more and more on the plectrum style. Having said that, even a brief listen to certain guitar heroes – such as Mark Knopfler (who always plays his electric with a fine fingerpicking style using just his thumb and 1st finger), John Lee Hooker (the master of the basic electric boogie), Johnny Marr or country-picking supremo Albert Lee – reveals how much more expression and variety good right hand technique allows.

Simple right hand fingerpicking patterns

Place an E major chord shape and try out these basic right hand patterns. You should have a gentle curve in the wrist so that the right hand fingers are almost at 90 degrees to the strings.

Keep your thumb straight and almost parallel to the strings. Use the tips of your fingers to play the strings. The overall position of the right hand is important. It should sit just over the half of the soundhole nearest the bridge to give a full, rounded tone. Some players do rest the hand on the guitar, but we recommend that you get used to holding your right hand in position free of any support.

Use the thumb to play the bottom string notes, while the index, middle and ring fingers pluck the 3rd, 2nd and 1st strings, respectively.

The perfect wrist position to begin fingerpicking.

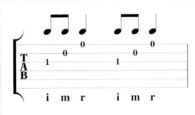

A simple pattern using just the three fingers.

Now add a bass note. Notice that the bass note is played by the thumb and falls on the 1st beat of the bar.

A simple arpeggio pattern with an alternating bass note. Keep the bass note on the beat.

Pluck the top three strings together, with an even pulling motion and an alternating bass line.

If these patterns feel a little difficult at first, don't be too concerned – you can refer back to them later. As you master each one, try it with the other full chords (not power chords) that you've learnt so far. Link the chords in new sequences and listen to the different effects that the same right hand pattern can create with different chords.

THE C MAJOR SCALE CHORD SEQUENCE

An explanation of 'primary' chords, the 'I, IV, V' chords that have a close musical relationship and often dominate entire songs.

Much of the chord theory covered on page 83 and the major scale theory exaplined on pages 81-81 will be brought together in this article. It might seem daunting at first, but it's actually a simple system. First, look back at page 81 to revise the major scale in the key of C and the construction of the C major chord.

Primary chords for C major

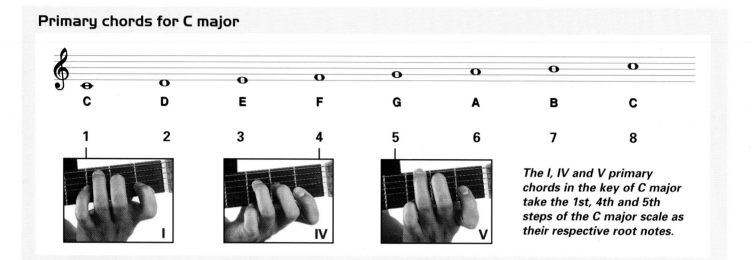

The I, IV and V primary chords in the key of C major take the 1st, 4th and 5th steps of the C major scale as their respective root notes.

The primary chords – I, IV, V

In any major key there are three chords that have a particularly close musical relationship and are often used together to form chord sequences in whole pieces of music. These 'primary' chords are all built using the 1st, 4th and 5th steps (or degrees) of their major scale as their root note. In the case of C major, the notes at those degrees in the scale are C, F and G, giving us the primary chords of C major, F major and G major.

Each of these primary chords is given a Roman numeral as a way of clearly differentiating them from the number names given to single notes in a scale. These chords are also given descriptive names that reflect their relationship to the key.

What is a key?

The key of any piece of music is derived from the particular scale that its notes tend towards overall, even if there might be some notes or chords that don't fit. The key, or tonic, note and therefore the tonic (I) chord will occur frequently – often at the beginning and end of a sequence. For example, The Animal's *The House Of The Rising Sun* relies heavily on its tonic chord of A minor, and Eric Clapton's *Wonderful Tonight*, which is in the key of G, has a similar reliance on the G chord.

For the key of C major:

C is **I**. It is also called the 'tonic' (from tone) chord.
F is **IV**. It is also called the 'sub-dominant' chord.
G is **V**. It is also called the 'dominant' chord.

The step V chord is sometimes played as a V7. In this case, it is G dominant 7, which is a new, but familiar sounding, chord. The word 'dominant' is usually dropped from its title it is just called G7. The note that makes it a '7' is the F, which is played on the 1st fret of the top E string.

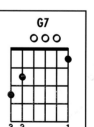

The G7 chord.

Primary structure

The relationship of these chords to one another provides a type of structure. The order in which they are played alters their effect; the move from the dominant chord G to the tonic has a strong effect, called a 'perfect cadence'. Try playing the chord sequences at the top of the next page. Note the effect of the G chord and how it sounds, as though it needs to return, or 'resolve', to C to finish.

C – F – C – G – C – F – G – C

or

C – G – C – F – G – G7 – C

The way that the I, IV and V chords are formed is the same for every key, just as it was in the construction of major chords (page 83) and scales (page 81). This table, which uses chords you already know, shows the I, IV and V chords for three different keys – A, D and G major. They are arrived at in exactly the same way as those in the key of C major, i.e. the I, IV and V chords take the 1st, 4th and 5th degree notes, respectively, as their root notes.

Primary chords for C, A, D and G major			
	I TONIC	IV SUB-DOMINANT	V (V7) DOMINANT (7TH)
KEY OF C	C	F	G (G7)
KEY OF A	A	D	E (E7)
KEY OF D	D	G	A (A7)
KEY OF G	G	C	D (D7)

With repetitions and variations in the order the chords appear, some kind of I, IV, V sequence is at the heart of every Blues, rock and country tune. As such, its importance can't be overstated – with these three chords, the basic form of thousands of songs can be played.

Building blocks

Buddy Holly (right), to name but one, based his entire oeuvre on this sequence. *Peggy Sue*, for example, is a cycle of C, F, C, G, C – in other words, I, IV, I, V, I. This also applies to early Beatles' music, much of The Stones, The Ramones, Chuck Berry and many, many more.

The majority of songs have used a I, IV, V sequence in some way. Some clear examples are: *I Saw Her Standing There* (The Beatles), *Wonderful Tonight*, and *Babies (by Pulp)*. *The Riverboat Song* (Ocean Colour Scene) and *Fake Plastic Trees* (Radiohead)also use a I, IV, V structure with some distinct adaptations.

Even if a song does not adhere strictly to primary chords in sequence, the deviations from it will be very significant. Therefore, it's an invaluable skill to recognize and understand the workings of primary chords, and how to find them when you need to play them.

All the scale tone chords for C major

The I, IV and V chords do not exist in isolation. There are, as you'd expect, equivalent chords in a major scale for every degree. Chords based on a scale in this way are called 'scale tone' chords. As with the I, IV and V chords, they each take a note of the scale as their root note. The chords need two other notes to be complete. Remember how the C major chord in Issue pages 81-82 is made up of the 1st, 3rd and 5th degrees of the C major scale? The scale tone chords are also completed with the notes found at the 3rd and 5th degrees up the C major scale from their name note. (N.B. These groupings that we keep coming across of three notes that make up chords are called 'triads'). This produces a pattern of major, minor and 'diminished' chords which is the same for every major key.

Below are all the scale tone chords for the key of C major. Some of them are unfamiliar to you, so use this chart as a reference.

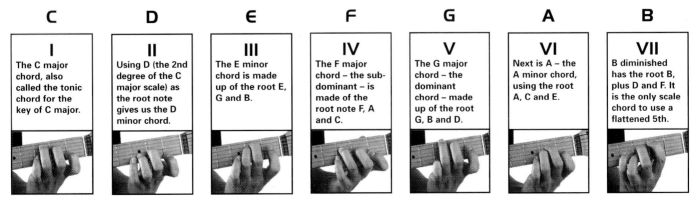

C	D	E	F	G	A	B
I The C major chord, also called the tonic chord for the key of C major.	**II** Using D (the 2nd degree of the C major scale) as the root note gives us the D minor chord.	**III** The E minor chord is made up of the root E, G and B.	**IV** The F major chord – the sub-dominant – is made of the root note F, A and C.	**V** The G major chord – the dominant chord – made up of the root G, B and D.	**VI** Next is A – the A minor chord, using the root A, C and E.	**VII** B diminished has the root B, plus D and F. It is the only scale chord to use a flattened 5th.

THE BARRE E AND A CHORDS

Explaining a sophisticated left hand skill – how to play barre chords – with a close look at two of the most commonly barred shapes.

Once mastered, barre chords make it simple to find the chord for any note with minimal change in finger shape, affording a great deal of flexibility in fretboard positions. In addition, some chords can be played only with the barring technique. Bare chords are a staple part of most playing styles are are particularly prevalent in rock music, where they facilitate rhythm guitar techniques such as rocking bass notes. Barre chords are difficult at first because they involve some hand strength, even on a guitar with an easy action. Keep practising and soon they'll become second nature.

Commonly barred shapes
Most chord shapes can be barred. However, barring works best with chords that don't require big finger stretches, as the barre itself leaves only three fingers with which to fret the chord shape. The simple and compact shapes of E and A and their minor and seventh versions are particularly suitable, as they all have a span of no more than three frets (including open strings). All barre chords require a good thumb position – straight behind the neck – to give your hand the maximum leverage and strength.

Consistent qualities
Wherever a barre chord is played, the intervals between each string remain the same. As a result, the chord will retain its particular qualities. A chord shape that makes

---

Barre chords
In a barre chord, finger 1 is used to form a barre across all the strings, effectively becoming a mobile top nut or capo. The remaining fingers form a chord shape above this finger, retaining the same distance in frets from the barre as they had from the top nut when played in 1st position.

We have occasionally referred to 'bar chords' before, which is a common shorthand used by some players. Since we will be using the term regularly from now on, we will use the correct spelling of the term – 'barre' (which is the French word for bar) to differentiate it clearly from a bar of music.

Barre chords are denoted in chord boxes as shown on the right. The barre itself is also sometimes shown as a curved or solid line.

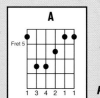

An A chord – a barred E shape in 5th position.

When every string of a full barre chord is being played, it looks like this in TAB. There is a number on every line, and there are no zeros to denote any open strings.

The A chord above as it would appear written in TAB.

The barred E shape
To make a barre E, the usual 1st position E chord shape is fretted with fingers 2, 3 and 4, which leaves finger 1 free to form the barre across all the strings at any position on the neck.

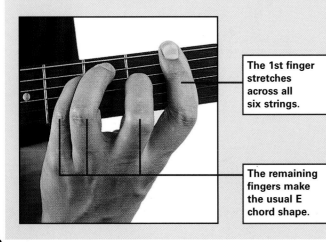

The 1st finger stretches across all six strings.

The remaining fingers make the usual E chord shape.

The barred A shape
More difficult than the E shape, the barred A shape can be played with just finger 3 fretting the D, G and B strings, two frets up from the barre. However, this doesn't suit everyone's fingers and it is more advisable to begin with the four-fingered version.

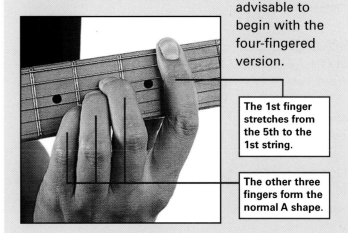

The 1st finger stretches from the 5th to the 1st string.

The other three fingers form the normal A shape.

a major chord in 1st position will always be a major chord when barred anywhere else, a minor chord shape will stay minor and a 7th chord shape will stay 7th. For example: an A minor shape barred at the 2nd fret becomes B minor and an A major shape barred at the 2nd fret will become B major.

Moving the barre chord shape

By moving the barre chord shape to different fret positions, you can make new chords. There's an easy way to work out the names of these new chords. Any barred E shape is referred to by the name of the note that the barre frets on the E strings. For example, the E shape becomes an F chord when barred at fret 1, an F sharp chord when barred at fret 2, a G chord at fret 3 and so on.

This also applies to barre A shapes. The chord will have the same name as the note being fretted on the A string. For example, the A shape becomes a B flat chord when barred at fret 1 and a B chord when barred at fret 2.

To change from a barre E to a barre A in the same position, move the barre up one string, and form the new shape with the other three fingers. (Some players keep the barre in place, omitting to play the 6th string in the A shape).

Primary chord theory

Refer back to the feature on primary chords (pages 88-89). Changing from a barred E shape to a barred A shape is similar to moving from an E chord to an A chord in 1st position, or from tonic to subdominant, or I to IV. In addition, a barred A shape played two frets up from its starting point provides the dominant (or V) chord. Thus, with a movement of only two fret positions, these two barre shapes give a player the facility to play a full I, IV, V sequence for any key. This, along with their strong, full sound, is what makes barre chords so prevalent in rock.

Different positions

One useful aspect of barre chords is that they offer a variety of different playing positions for the same chord, allowing economy of movement. For example, a G chord can be played as a barred E shape in 3rd position or a barred A shape in 10th position. The latter would be preferable if you were playing high up the neck, whereas the former would be handy if you were playing around 3rd position.

Barre chords and punk

The front page of a punk fanzine published in 1976 called *Sniffin' Glue* carried three chord boxes showing C, F and G chords, accompanied by the challenge, 'Here's three chords – now go and form a band'. As minimal as this might seem, the truth was that the majority of punk guitarists began by learning only one or two chord shapes – E and A. Just by barring one shape at different places on the neck, they could play the major chord of any note with a consistent, powerful sound. The Ramones were prime exponents of this art, as were The Undertones. The glorious riff from the latter's debut (and, incidentally, John Peel's all-time favourite single) *Teenage Kicks*, is built entirely around barred E chords moved down and up the neck.

Damian O'Neill – rhythm guitarist with The Undertones – playing a barre E7 shape.

SUSSING OUT SEVENTHS

An explanation and examination of two particular types of chord

The names might appear complex, but sevenths are based on the same logical system as that used for major and minor chords.

It's a great asset for a player to be able to recognize the effect these chords have and how they are formed.

Take the time to understand them now, and they will seem less intimidating. The relevant chords are shown in the key of D throughout, but remember that the rules for building chords apply to every key.

MAJOR, MINOR AND POWER CHORD CONSTRUCTION (a reminder)

To recap the theory behind major, minor and power chords, refer back to pages 81-85.

Power chords (D5)

All power chords (or '5 chords) are made up of just the 1st and 5th steps of their major scale, hence their name.

The D power chord, formed by just the root note, D, and A (5th).

Major chords (D major)

All major chords are made up of the 1st, 3rd and 5th steps of the major scale, often with the 1st and 5th repeated in octaves.

The 1st position D major chord is made up of an open D, A, D repeated an octave above, and (on the top string) F#, which is the 3rd step of the major scale.

Minor chords (D minor)

All minor chords are made up of the 1st, 3rd and 5th notes of their minor scale, again often with the root note and 5th as octaves.

For a D minor chord, we have D (the root note), A (the 5th), D repeated an octave above, and F (the minor 3rd).

The D major and D natural minor scales

The diagram below shows the D major scale (top) and the D natural minor scale (bottom) in notation. Natural minor scales were introduced in Issue 12; their sequence of intervals (or distances between notes) is T S T T S T T (T = tone, or two frets, S = semitone, or one fret).

A comparison of these two scales reveals that there is a semitone difference between both the major and minor 3rd and the major and minor 7th, and that the 2nd, 4th and 5th steps are the same notes in both scales. The notes that form the chords on the opposite page can all be found in the relevant major or minor scale.

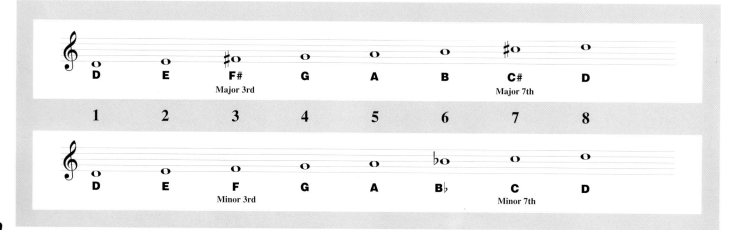

7TH CHORDS
7th chords are made up of the major or minor triad plus the 7th note from the relevant scale.

The major 7th (D major 7 or Dmaj7)
Major 7th chords are distinguished by their jazzy, sweet sound. Like major chords, they are based on the root note, the major 3rd and the 5th. The additional major 7th note, one semitone down from the octave, gives the chord its melodious quality. D major 7 (pictured below), can be formed by barring the top three strings.

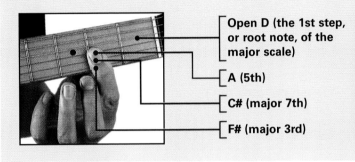

Open D (the 1st step, or root note, of the major scale)

A (5th)

C# (major 7th)

F# (major 3rd)

The minor 7th (D minor 7 or Dm7)
Minor 7ths are characterized by their wistful, melancholic quality – slightly more sophisticated than straight minor chords. This is because they not only contain the 1st, minor 3rd and 5th of minor chords but also the minor 7th above the root note. Below is a breakdown of the D minor 7 chord.

Open D (the 1st step, or root note, of the minor scale)

A (5th)

C (minor 7th)

F (minor 3rd)

7th, or dominant 7th chords
To help you get to grips with these chords, refer back to pages 88-89. Although they should strictly be called dominant 7ths, these chords are (confusingly) just referred to as 7ths. They work differently from the two 7th chords above, in that they have an almost 'weak' quality when not combined with the key chord. Since D7 is the dominant 7th chord in the key of G major, it consists of notes taken from that scale, and is generally followed by a G major chord. Although the only place that we've used these 7 chords was on pages 88-89, they are one of the many hallmarks of rock'n'roll and the Blues, a subject that we will deal with later in greater depth.

The 1st position D7 chord.

SUSPENDED CHORDS
These suspended chords are built, like major or minor chords, from a triad, with a 2nd or 4th note in place of a major or minor 3rd. This substituted note gives them their suspended, hanging quality.

Suspended 4ths, or 'sus4' (Dsus4)
Sus4s are formed from the 1st, 4th and 5th steps of the major or minor scale. When playing Dsus4, changing from the 4th note, G at fret 3 on the top E, to the major 3rd note, F# at the 2nd fret, 'resolves' the chord into a straight D major. The switch between these two is very common in rock and pop guitar playing.

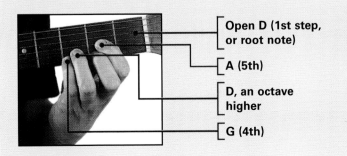

Open D (1st step, or root note)

A (5th)

D, an octave higher

G (4th)

Suspended 2nds, or 'sus2' (Dsus2)
These work in a similar way to sus4 chords. The 2nd step takes the place of the major 3rd. Moving the 2nd note back to the major 3rd turns a sus2 chord into a normal major chord, a trick used by Cast in this Issue's Songbook.The 1st position sus2 chords of A and D both incorporate open strings, and players often use them for their resultant ringing quality.

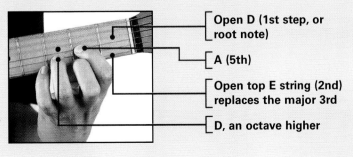

Open D (1st step, or root note)

A (5th)

Open top E string (2nd) replaces the major 3rd

D, an octave higher

LINES AND SPACES

How to read the pitch of notes from their position on a stave.

The last time we dealt with reading notation was on 78-79, which concentrated exclusively on the timing values of notes. Have that article to hand for reference, in case there are any aspects of timing of which you are unsure.

We have only been using notation symbols as a method of providing the essential information that the TAB cannot give (ie: the rhythm values of the notes). As a result, these symbols have been shown floating free.

But normally, notes are deliberately positioned on a stave, which allows notation to provide all the required information about both the timing and pitch.

The stave

The most recent use of a full notation stave has been to demonstrate major and minor scales. Below is a recap of the notation stave and how it works.

Representing pitch

The treble clef

Most guitar music is written in the treble clef. This symbol is derived from an ancient version of the letter G. The line that this 'squiggle' coils around represents the note G above middle C. (Middle C is a useful reference point for pitch, and is named after the C key found in the middle of a piano's keyboard.) To make it visually easier, guitar music is written in notation an octave below its actual pitch – but don't let that confuse you!

Lines and spaces

Unlike TAB, a stave has only five lines. The lines of TAB directly mirror the strings of a guitar, whereas a stave is a more abstract representation of pitch. Each line and each space in between stands for a different letter note. The names of those notes are shown in the stave below.

Timing symbols

Time signature

This symbol appears on the first stave, next to the treble clef (refer back to pages 78-9 for more info). Many rock pieces are in $\frac{4}{4}$ which means that each bar has a value of four beats (the number above) and that these are crotchet beats (represented by the lower 4).

Bar lines

These vertical lines mark the beginning and end of each bar of music – in $\frac{4}{4}$ each group of notes and rests add up to a count of four.

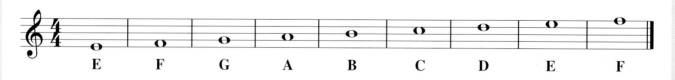

E   F   G   A   B   C   D   E   F

One symbol that does not occur in this stave is the group of flats or sharps called the key signature. Written to the right of the clef, each flat or sharp symbol in the group tells you which notes must be flattened or sharpened by its position on the stave.

Altogether, these symbols help identify the key of the piece. The pieces in this article are all in the key of C, which contains no sharps or flats. Individual flats or sharps can also be shown as 'accidentals' – symbols that are placed to the left of the relevant note.

Finding notes on the fretboard

The stave below shows a full octave, from bottom E to top E, written out in standard notation. The accompanying photographs show where you'll find each of these notes in 1st position.

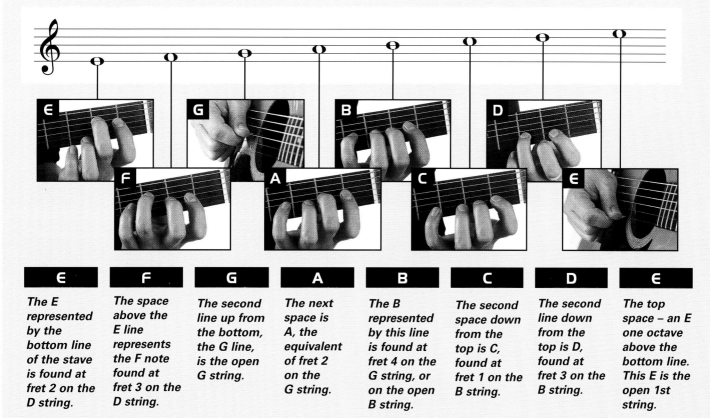

E	F	G	A	B	C	D	E
The E represented by the bottom line of the stave is found at fret 2 on the D string.	*The space above the E line represents the F note found at fret 3 on the D string.*	*The second line up from the bottom, the G line, is the open G string.*	*The next space is A, the equivalent of fret 2 on the G string.*	*The B represented by this line is found at fret 4 on the G string, or on the open B string.*	*The second space down from the top is C, found at fret 1 on the B string.*	*The second line down from the top is D, found at fret 3 on the B string.*	*The top space – an E one octave above the bottom line. This E is the open 1st string.*

Note stems

The stave below shows two other variables that occur in notation. The piece moves from two-count minims in the first two bars to four-count semibreves in the last two bars. The minims are mainly differentiated from the semibreves by their stems.

Notice that the stems of the 1st three minims point upwards, whereas that of the 4th points down. This makes no difference to the note itself, it's simply a question of how notes are written for neatness in standard practice. The rule is as follows: stemmed notes that occur below the B line are written with stems that point upwards, while those above this middle line are given stems that point downwards.

Sight-reading

Try playing the following string of notes which dispenses with bars to concentrate on recognizing pitch alone. We haven't given the names of the notes, so if you're unsure of where any note is to be found, you'll have to use the photographs and stave at the top of the page as a visual reminder. A great aid to learning is to say the name of the note just before you play it. Every note is written as a semibreve, but take as long as you need to recognize and play each note in order. Only notes from G to D have been included.

TUNING AROUND

A guide to some of the more commonly used alternative tunings.

Ry Cooder, a master of slide guitar playing, uses a variety of open tunings.

Conventional E A D G B E tuning provides a reasonable range with fairly easy fingerings for most basic chords. However, many traditional styles of folk and Blues (especially 'bottleneck' or slide playing) make use of alternative tunings.

Alternative tunings necessitate different fingerings for chords and scales. For some players, altered tunings are an integral part of their guitar style. Others simply use them as a means of finding inspiration – the tunings create surprising effects and each demands a different approach to playing.

There are two basic types of alternative tunings: open tunings, in which playing all the open strings together produces a chord; and partial adaptations of standard tuning, which allow players to use the ringing sound of one or two particular open strings.

Open tunings

In open tuning, basic chords can be played with a finger barre across all six strings. In open G, for example, a barre at fret 2 gives the chord A. This also facilitates slide and bottleneck playing, as the slide can be used like a barre. Having the open chord as a simple major or minor chord offers plenty of variation.

For open G you need to re-tune only three strings. (**Note:** Keith Richards' habit of removing the 6th string when in open G needn't bother you – you can simply tune the string down to D, to give a low 5th.) Take a look at the chart below.

A barre at fret 2 makes an A chord in open G.

1st position C chord in open G.

Open G	
1st	down to D
2nd	normal (B)
3rd	normal (G)
4th	normal (D)
5th	down to G
6th	down to D

1st position G chord in open D.

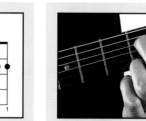

1st position A7 chord in open D.

Open D	
1st	down to D
2nd	normal (B)
3rd	down to F#
4th	normal (D)
5th	normal (A)
6th	down to D

Open E and open C tunings, traditionally used for folk-Blues, both require some strings to be pitched higher than in standard tuning. If you wish to try this, you might want to use a lighter gauge string than normal.

Open E	
1st	normal (E)
2nd	normal (B)
3rd	up to G#
4th	up to E
5th	up to B
6th	normal (E)

Open C	
1st	normal (E)
2nd	up to C
3rd	normal (G)
4th	down to C
5th	down to G
6th	down to C

Minor or 'crossnote' tunings

These are, as you would expect, essentially the same as major tunings, with the major 3rd of the chord flattened to make it minor. To return to the open E major chord, simply fret the 3rd string at fret 1 – or in the case of a barred chord, barre all the strings with the 1st finger and add finger 2 a fret higher on string 3.

Open D minor	
1st	down to D
2nd	normal (B)
3rd	down to F
4th	normal (D)
5th	normal (A)
6th	down to D

Open E minor	
1st	normal (E)
2nd	normal (B)
3rd	normal (G)
4th	up to E
5th	up to B
6th	normal (E)

Modal tunings

The open strings of a 'modally' tuned guitar will make a suspended 4th chord. It's a tuning common in intricate fingerpicking styles, as it makes possible particularly pleasing variations between closed and open strings.

D modal	
1st	down to D
2nd	down to A
3rd	normal (G)
4th	normal (D)
5th	normal (A)
6th	down to D

G modal	
1st	down to D
2nd	up to C
3rd	normal (G)
4th	normal (D)
5th	down to G
6th	down to D

Dropped tunings

These involve dropping the pitch of only one or two strings from standard tuning. In dropped D tuning you can alternate between two open string D notes, an octave apart, for a strong,

Dropped D	
1st	normal (E)
2nd	B or A
3rd	normal (G)
4th	normal (D)
5th	normal (A)
6th	down to D

rhythmic effect.

Dropped D is also useful for playing in the keys of D and A, since the 5th string can act as the bass note for A and the open 6th provides the lower bass note for the sub-dominant chord of D.

Miscellaneous tunings

Alternatively, just tuning in the conventional way, but to a lower pitch, can produce pleasant, mellow-sounding chords. Many early Blues players tuned their guitars low, with the top and bottom strings tuned down to C instead of the conventional E. A less musicianly approach is to tune all the strings to the same note and then play barre or slide fingerings with only one finger! This highly effective 'cheat' was a trick deployed in the 'Seventies by 'glam' monsters The Glitter Band, as it is a very easy way to create simple, powerful-sounding riffs, especially if played on a distorted electric. Kid Congo Powers, lead guitarist with The Cramps, The Gun Club, Nick Cave's Bad Seeds and currently Congo Norvell, has always played this way, with great success.

Tuning hints – limits and problems

There are practical limitations to alternative tunings. Altering the pitch of any one string can affect the others by changing the overall stresses in the guitar and possibly the pitch of the other strings. This is especially true for electric guitars with a sprung tremolo bridge. As a result, you should check the tuning of all six strings even if you have de-tuned only one. Using a modified version of relative tuning (see pages 40-41) is inadequate – you really need some reference point. A chromatic tuner is an invaluable aid if you intend to alter tunings regularly.

Lowering the pitch of strings, as in open tunings, is safer and easier than raising it. Some alternative tunings do involve raising the pitch, but be aware that without changing to lighter gauge strings this places extra stress on both the guitar and the string itself, possibly leading to the string breaking or even damage to the guitar. An extreme example is Robert Fripp's New Standard Tuning, which features both very low de-tuned bass strings and extremely high top strings; from low to high, this radically different tuning is C G D A E G. It causes extreme changes in stress on a guitar, so instruments played in this tuning require both modification and custom sets of strings.

BENDING AND SHAKING

Examining the variations of these essential left hand techniques.

Both vibrato and string bends are particularly prevalent in Blues and rock electric solo playing, but they are also relevant to acoustic players. Classical and flamenco guitar players, for example, use vibrato, although they rarely play string bends.

Above and beyond all considerations of equipment and effects, it's with his fretting style that each player makes his unique sound. Learning to use these techniques with the minimum force and the maximum effect is a matter of practising until they become second nature. Eric Clapton insists that the calibre of a player should be gauged by the lightness of their touch – the ability to play with just the effort required and no more is the sign of a master.

VIBRATO
Vibrato (the Italian word for 'vibrated') is one of the most expressive guitar techniques and is relevant to all styles of playing. Fast but tiny movements of the fretting hand or finger produce oscillations in the note, and this has the added effect of drawing out the natural sustain of a note. When subtly applied, it is highly effective, but beware of relying on vibrato to add intensity to otherwise unimaginative solos.

There is no single correct vibrato technique, as it depends very much on a player's style and the strength of his or her hands, wrist and fingers. BB King generates his fast vibrato by rapidly rotating the hand at the wrist, while Eric Clapton releases his thumb from the neck entirely, leaving only the fretting finger to pivot on the string with the force of his hand behind it. Some rock guitar players shake the whole guitar to get vibrato, or simply use their tremolo arm. Broadly speaking, however, there are two main approaches to vibrato: either side to side or up and down.

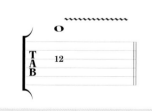
Vibrato as it appears in TAB.

Side-to-side vibrato
Many players use this technique when they wish to create a slow vibrato. The fretted finger is rolled from left to right but the tip of the finger remains in the same place. This movement comes from both the wrist and the forearm, with the elbow as a static leverage point. The changes in pressure on the string due to this rolling motion produce small fluctuations in the note's pitch, giving the vibrato effect.

Side-to-side vibrato.

Up-and-down vibrato
This technique is used on *Sunshine Of Your Love* by Cream. The fretting finger pushes the string up and down in a series of rapid, tiny string bends. You can do this by pivoting the left hand at the wrist, but some players use the strength of each individual finger.

Up-and-down vibrato.

STRING BENDS
The bend is one of the identifying sounds of steel string guitar playing. It was originally employed to imitate the 'blue' notes of Blues slide guitar and country pedal steel. The prevalence of string bending in modern guitar playing has led to the development of lighter and lighter strings, which make bends easier.

Using the 3rd finger gives your hand the most leverage for a bend. The 1st and 2nd fingers can be just as effective, but the 4th finger is usually too weak. The 2nd and 3rd strings are physically the easiest to bend (either up or down) due to their position on the fretboard. The lower strings are harder to bend, due to both position and gauge. When bending the lower strings, these need to be pulled towards the upper strings to avoid pushing them off the fretboard.

Allowing your thumb to slip up over the top of the fretboard gives the extra leverage your hand requires. This also applies to some vibrato techniques. The knack of good bending is accuracy, which can be accomplished only by regular practice. Playing the fretted note that you wish to achieve before attempting it with the bend gives your ear a reference point.

Upward bends

Strike the string and then bend it up a semitone (the equivalent of one fret), a whole tone (the equivalent of two frets), or even further where possible.

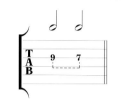

A common 3rd string bend.

Downward bends

These are standard bends in reverse. The string has already been bent when it is struck, and the bend is then released.

The same bend as above, only in reverse.

Unison bends

Bending the 3rd string up until it matches a higher fretted note on the 2nd string is a common technique in rock and Blues. This technique, which can be applied to any of the strings but works best on the top three, is known as 'unison bending'.

Unison 3rd string bends are instantly recognizable as part of rock music. This one is played in 5th position.

Advanced bends – double string bends

Often in Blues or rock'n'roll playing, the 2nd and 3rd strings are bent together to produce a strong Bluesy effect. The finger and string position mean that the 2nd string gets bent up a semitone while the 3rd is bent up by a whole tone.

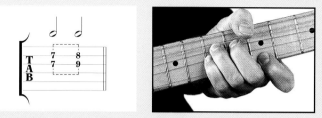

Difficult to play at first, this strong-sounding double string bend is a hallmark of Chuck Berry's style.

Advanced bends – a country bend

A similar technique to that used in a unison bend can be employed to create this bend.

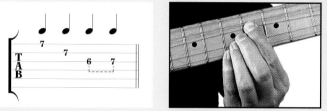

To play this country-sounding figure, pick the top two strings before making a semitone bend on the 3rd string.

BENDS ON ACOUSTICS
Bends are noticeably more difficult on the heavier strings of acoustics. Some acoustic players opt for an unwound 3rd string, which makes 3rd string bends easier.

Combining bends and vibrato

These techniques can be combined for extra effect. One excellent combination uses vibrato at the end of an upward or downward bend. Guitarists Tom Verlaine and BB King employ this trick, but with completely different results.

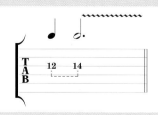

Bending the 3rd string at fret 12 up to 14th fret pitch before adding vibrato.

The exercise below is a solo flourish that involves four techniques in sequence. Perform the upward bend, then add vibrato, before releasing the note with a downward bend, and then finishing with a quick slide up two frets.

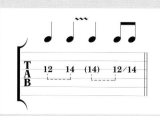

The photo shows the end of the upward slide in this four-part flourish.

THE MINOR PENTATONIC SCALE

Examining a scale with a daunting name that is actually easy to master, and which will set you on the road to soloing.

The pentatonic scale, which forms the basis of all Eastern, African and Celtic music, is thought to have originated thousands of years ago in Mongolia or Japan. This common root is one of the reasons why world music combinations of African and Blues or jazz and Indian styles, for example, can work so well. There are two basic forms of the pentatonic scale – major and minor. Each uses five notes from the major and minor scales, respectively, hence the name – 'pent', from the Greek word *pente* for five.

The minor pentatonic

Minor pentatonic scales form the basis of the great majority of Blues and rock. Every minor pentatonic scale is made up of the 1st, 3rd, 4th, 5th and 7th notes of a natural minor scale. These notes fit over most simple rock chord progressions, especially I, IV and V sequences (see pages 88–89).

	A	B	C	D	E	F	G	A
				0	2	3	0	2
TAB	0	2	3					
	1	2	3	4	5	6	7	8

The natural A minor scale, from Issue 12, with the steps that form the A minor pentatonic highlighted within it.

Fingering patterns

A common way of mastering scales is to learn them as manageable chunks in the form of moveable 'patterns'. These patterns tend to have a span of around four frets, which allows the left hand to stay in one position per pattern. In addition, they are easy to visualize (and therefore memorize). The trick to using such patterns is knowing where the root note of the scale occurs. This enables you to find the right fret position to play a pattern in the required key.

The minor pentatonic pattern shown here has its root note at the 1st finger position on the bottom E string, the 3rd finger position (two frets up) on the D string and the 1st finger position on the top E string. When played at the 5th fret, these notes are all A. In this position, the pattern forms an A minor pentatonic scale.

This pattern starts in 5th position and spans four frets. Play all the fret 5 notes with the 1st finger, the fret 7 notes with finger 3 and all the fret 8 notes with finger 4. Try to 'walk' your fingers up and down the pattern until you become familiar with its shape. The root note positions are circled in white.

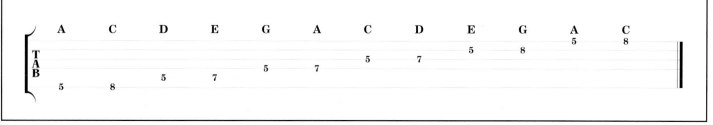

	A	C	D	E	G	A	C	D	E	G	A	C
											5	8
									5	8		
TAB							5	7				
				5	7							
	5	8	5									

The A minor pentatonic shown in TAB, starting on the bottom E string at fret 5 and working upwards.

Jamming along

On the right are some licks taken from the 5th position A minor pentatonic pattern for you to try. It's important to recognize when you are playing a root note, so watch out and listen for several occurrences of the root note A in these examples.

Once you've got the hang of the pentatonic scale, try making up your own solos from the same A minor pattern. If you find the choice of notes bewildering, begin by using those found on the top three strings only, using a simple, repetitive rhythm, such as a crotchet and two quavers. Remember that there's no limit to the number of times a note from the pattern can be repeated. The same note with an interesting rhythm pattern can be just as effective as a chain of different notes. Try playing from the low notes up, from the high notes down and a combination of both. Large pitch leaps can work well – it all depends on the effect you want to achieve.

Using any of the three licks suggested here as a starting point. Listen carefully to the effect of the selection and timing of each note that you play, and aim to extend your range gradually until you are using notes from all over the pattern.

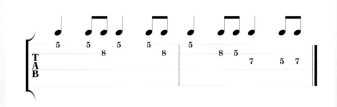

This phrase takes notes found on the top three strings only and makes use of the root note on the top string.

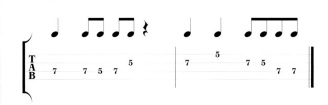

This lick begins and ends on the root note A.

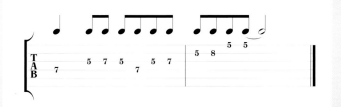

A solo that moves from the 4th string up to the 1st.

Different positions

It's important to understand that every pattern can be moved to any other position for playing in a different key. For example, shifting the 5th position pattern down two frets to 3rd position gives you a G minor pentatonic scale. This is suitable for jamming over a track in G as all the notes in the pattern's root note positions will now be G. Moving the whole pattern up to 8th position gives you a C minor pentatonic scale, and so on.

Link to the Blues

Minor pentatonic scales offer limited scope for improvisation, but they are an important starting point. With the addition of some extra notes – a flattened 5th, an optional major 6th and 2nd – they become Blues scales. These offer greater melodic possibilities for soloing. The next feature on this subject will look at a full Blues scale and how to incorporate some left hand techniques into your improvisation.

The A minor pentatonic scale up to fret 13

The A minor pentatonic scale can be played in five different patterns that link up along the entire length of the neck. Each one has a slightly different tonality and effect due to their different position. The knack

of linking these patterns smoothly without sudden leaps in left hand position is something that only comes with practice. Refer back to this diagram as you begin learning these patterns by heart.

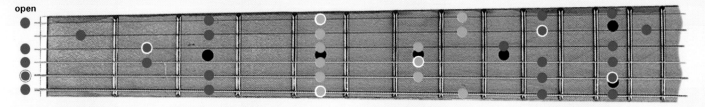

Three linking patterns that can be used to play the A minor pentatonic scale up to the 13th fret. Every root note (in this case A) in each pattern is marked by a white ring.

The 5th position pattern is highlighted. The first two patterns repeat above the 12th fret. These patterns can be played at any fret position, according to the desired key.

BLUES SCALES AND BEYOND

How to transform the minor pentatonic with just a few extra notes.

The scales shown on these pages are only a few of the scales available to improvise with. There are also modal scales, whole tone scales, and diminished and augmented scales. Although these are often associated with jazz, the more adventurous rock player can also take soloing to new heights by investigating them.

Linking minor pentatonic patterns

The three examples of A minor pentatonic soloing on the previous pages were each taken from just one pattern. However, constructing solos from linked sequences of more than one pattern will produce much more fluent and expressive results. After this, the next step is to work on incorporating left hand techniques into your lead breaks.

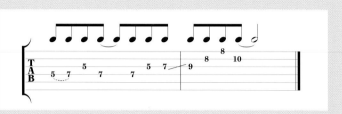

This two-pattern lick incorporates two left hand techniques: a hammer-on from fret 5 to fret 7 on the D string and a slide from fret 7 to fret 9 on the G string.

The Blues scale

This is one of the most used (or overused) scales in rock'n'roll, pop and Blues music. It can be played over a I, IV, V chord sequence, and is based around the the minor pentatonic scale with the addition of a flattened 5th (the scale's standard 5th note lowered by a semitone). This note is called a 'blue' note and is a characteristic of Blues and Blues-derived music. All the patterns for playing minor pentatonics can be modified into Blues scales by adding the flattened 5th, which in this case is E flat.

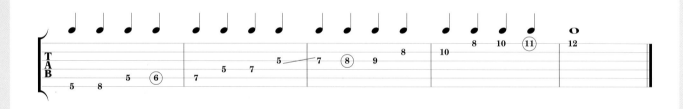

This Blues scale in A starts in 5th position. You should be able to recognize the A minor pentatonic scale at its core. The flattened 5th 'blue' notes have been circled. This scale can be played over a I, IV, V chord sequence in A.

A Blues scale pattern

Patterns are a convenient way of learning Blues scales. With the addition of the flattened 5th notes, they are the same as those used to play minor pentatonic scales.

There are some further optional additions to the basic Blues scale which increase its melodic possibilities. These include adding the major 3rd, which allows you to combine major harmony with the minor scale, and the major 2nd and major 6th. Usually played on the top three strings only, they bring a rich, jazzy quality to Blues solos, which is exemplified in the playing style of BB King.

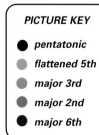

PICTURE KEY

● pentatonic

● flattened 5th

● major 3rd

● major 2nd

● major 6th

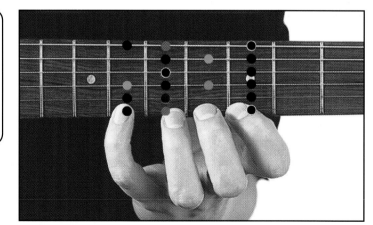

This pattern can be played in any position – the root notes are circled in white. In 5th position, as shown here, it forms a Blues scale in A. The optional extra major 3rd, 2nd and 6th are clearly marked, as is the Bluesy flattened 5th.

Bends in Blues and minor pentatonic scales

The left hand technique most closely associated with lead Blues playing is string bending. One commonly bent note is the 4th, which is pushed up a semitone until it reaches the equivalent of the flattened 5th of the Blues scale. Downward bends, pull-offs, staccato and vibrato are other techniques that are frequently used to bring Blues and minor pentatonic scales to life in lead playing.

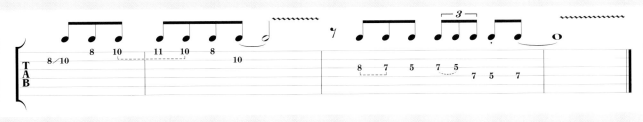

Use the A Blues scale and this lick to start your own solo, playing along with the CD 'jamming track' (Track 92).

The C major pentatonic scale

The minor pentatonic is fine for power chord and minor sequences, but to play solos in major keys you need to know the major pentatonic scale. The notes of this scale form the same patterns on the neck as the minor pentatonic, but the root notes are found at different places in the scale. A minor is the relative minor of C (see page 84-85), which means that the A minor pentatonic scale has the same notes as the C major pentatonic, and the patterns used to play both scales occur in the same places.

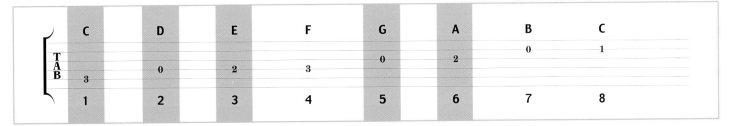

The C major scale with the steps that form the C major pentatonic scale highlighted within it.

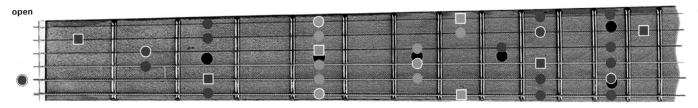

The three patterns that form the C major pentatonic and the A minor pentatonic up to the 13th fret. The root notes for the C scale are shown as highlighted squares, while those for the A minor pentatonic are circled.

Diatonic scales

Diatonic scales are full major and minor scales with a seven-note range. Because their range is greater than that of the pentatonic, there is more scope for the creation of melodic runs. As with pentatonic scale patterns, the major and its relative minor share the same pattern, but the root notes change position.

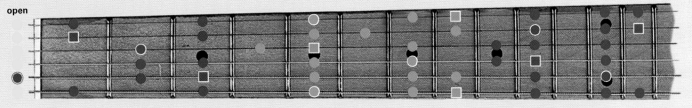

Three patterns up to the 12th fret that form the C major and A minor diatonic scales. As before, the root notes for C major are shown in squares, while those for the relative minor are circled.

KEY TO THE MUSIC

The keys that you have been playing in – and how to change them.

The western concept of 'key' emerged in the early 17th century. It evolved from the system of 'modes' – a limited system based on sequences of fixed intervals beginning at different notes. The key system, however, allows greater flexibility. Although a few experimental bands occasionally dispense with the now traditional concept of key, most rock, Blues, reggae, dance and folk songs are firmly rooted to their own particular key. In fact, our ears are so attuned to the effect of a key that we have come to expect one.

Definition of key

The key of a piece of music is defined by the scale to which its notes generally adhere. The piece doesn't have to include all the notes of a scale, but the majority of the scale's notes will usually be present. The overall sound that this gives to a piece of music is called its 'tonality'. A melody made up from notes found in the scale of C major is said to be in the key of C major, and this can be called the piece's 'key centre'. To use one song as an example, *The House Of The Rising Sun* has a chord sequence and melody that is based on the A minor scale, and is therefore in the key of A minor.

Not all the notes of a song have to derive from its key. However, most rock, pop, Blues and soul music relies very heavily on keys, especially their basic I, IV, V chord sequences.

Value for solos

One particular virtue of knowing the key of a song is that it gives you the root note for solos. Refer back to the pentatonic solo patterns that we featured on pages 100-103. If you wish to use pentatonic or other scale patterns to solo over a song, you must know what key you're in, as this will give you the root note and therefore the correct position for your patterns.

Six common keys

Most rock and pop songs are played in a limited number of keys. These correspond to the bottom four open strings, and that's one reason why they are so common – because they allow the use of chord shapes with open strings that can provide strong tonic notes. Chords in these keys also offer 'friendlier' finger shapes, which is another reason why the six keys listed in the chart below are the most commonly used.

Key of G	Scale: G A B C D E F# G	e.g. *Wonderful Tonight* – Eric Clapton, *There She Goes* – The La's, *On And On* – The Longpigs
Key of D	Scale: D E F# G A B C# D	e.g. *Babies* – Pulp, *Ironic* – Alanis Morissette, *The Bartender And The Thief* – Stereophonics, *Lump* – The Presidents Of The USA
Key of A	Scale: A B C# D E F# G# A	e.g. *I Saw Her Standing There* – The Beatles, *Fake Plastic Trees* – Radiohead, *Rocks* – Primal Scream, *Buffalo Soldier* – Bob Marley, *All Right Now* – Free
Key of E	Scale: E F# G# A B C# D# E	e.g. *And She Was* – Talking Heads, *One To Another* – The Charlatans, *Jailhouse Rock* – Elvis Presley, *That'll Be The Day* – Buddy Holly, *There Goes The Neighborhood* – Sheryl Crow, *Folsom Prison Blues* – Johnny Cash
E minor	relative minor of G	e.g. *Wonderwall* – Oasis, *Zombie* – The Cranberries
A minor	relative minor of C	e.g. *Wildwood* – Paul Weller, *The House Of The Rising Sun* – The Animals, *Staying Out For The Summer* – Dodgy

Finding the key

There are some short cuts to working out the key of a song. The majority of rock and pop songs begin and end on the key note chord. There are exceptions, however – *Jailhouse Rock,* for example, has a slurred chord of D sharp just before the main E chord – so don't assume too much. Try to train your ear to pick up subtle differences. You should also learn to distinguish between the melancholic mood of a song with an overall minor feel, such as *Wonderwall*, and the happier sound of a song with a major tonality, such as *There She Goes*.

Importance of the tonic

The effect of every other note and chord is determined by its relationship to the tonic, for this note gives a sense of key to the whole piece. Rock music tends to underline the key of a song with the repeated use of a solid chord based on the key note.

Keys in standard notation, and the 'cycle of 5ths'

The key of any piece of music is easy to spot when it is written in standard notation. In this system, the key is shown by a collection of flats or sharps at the beginning of the stave, called the key signature. Here are the key signatures for the six common guitar keys from the previous page. Natural minor scales share the same notes as their relative majors (see page 84), and they also therefore share

their relative major's key signatures. E minor has the same key signature as G, and A minor shares the key signature of C (shown left).

From l to r: the key signatures of G, D, A and E. Notice that a pattern emerges from these keys; each one is a 5th up from the last (in guitarist's language, an interval of seven frets) and each successive key has the same sharps as the previous key, plus a new one. This occurs because a sharp has to be added each time to keep the same intervals of the major scale – T T S T T T S (see page 81). This part of the peculiar logic of musical notation is called the 'cycle of 5ths'.

Transposition

Changing the key of a whole song or piece of music is called transposition. It is commonly done if the original key is too high or too low for a singer. The easiest method of transposing music to a higher key is to use a capo (see page 55). All the original fingerings move to a higher key according to the fret at which the capo is placed. For example, with a capo at fret 1, a 1st position C chord shape becomes a C sharp chord, the same chord becomes a D chord if the capo is at fret 2, and so on. Conversely, if a song is written with a capo to start off with, removing it will allow you to play the same chord sequence in a lower key.

Played without a capo, the original chord sequence of *Why Does It Always Rain On Me?* in 1st position will now be one tone lower – transposing the song to the actual key of D rather than its previous key of E. If you are singing along, you should now find the high notes easier to hit.

The TAB system also makes transposition relatively easy. As long as you remember to include open strings in your calculations, and also take potential fingering difficulties into account, simple pieces can easily be transposed by adding or subtracting the same number of frets to or from every tab number. For example: raising the key of a solo in G to A would involve adding two frets (that is, a whole tone) to every fret number.

Keeping the harmony

The crucial thing to remember when transposing is that you must preserve the harmony of each chord, which means that major and minor chords must remain major and minor, 7ths must remain 7ths, and so on.

C	D	E	F	G
Dm	Em	F#m	Gm	Am
G7	A7	B7	C7	D7
Cmaj7	Dmaj7	Emaj7	Fmaj7	Gmaj7

The highlighted sequence of chords in D has been transposed down to C on the left, and up to E, F and G on the right.

In the example above, each chord has kept its original 'flavour'. Barre chords will help you to do this, but so will learning all the chord shapes for every key in each position. A later article will provide a comprehensive guide to chords for every key.

Modulation

Songs can also include a change of key, called a modulation. This effect provides tonal variety. A modulation can be found in *Freak Scene* by Dinosaur Jr. The song has firmly established the key of D with a D (I), Em (II), A (V) chord sequence. After one verse and instrumental break, however, it shifts up a whole tone to the key of E major with E (I) and F sharp minor (II) chords, before returning to the original key.

TWO-HANDED TRICKS

Some more advanced left and right hand techniques with example licks.

Multiple pull-offs

Up to four fretted notes can be pulled-off in succession from one position to create descending flurries of notes. Players often use multiple pull-offs like these as a way of playing licks from pentatonic and Blues scales.

 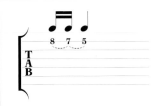

Pulling-off with the 4th and then the 3rd finger on the E string is a lick that's used in many Blues solos. The one shown here is based on a Blues scale in A.

Trills

A rapid succession of hammer-ons and pull-offs between two notes creates an effect called a trill. Extended trills are a common feature of rock and Blues solos. They create a hovering effect, and are often used before a run up or down a scale.

 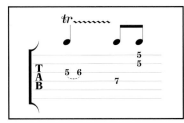

This lick, also in the key of A, begins with a trill between the 5th and the 6th fret on the G string.

 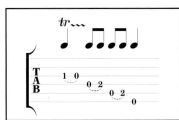

Try out this lick, which involves a trill at fret 1 on the G string, followed by a descent through notes from the E Blues scale.

Fretted string harmonics

Like open strings, fretted strings have harmonic points at even divisions – one-half, one-quarter, one-eighth, etc. – of their length. The easiest fretted harmonics to play are the half-length (or octave) ones for notes fretted up to the 9th or 10th fret, depending on the length of the fretboard. The halfway harmonic point is directly over the fret wire 12 frets higher. For example, the fret 5 note on the top E string (A) has an octave harmonic directly over the 17th fret. Finding the right spot for notes whose octave harmonics are 'off the fretboard' takes a little more judgement.

If using a plectrum, shift it quickly to your thumb and middle finger to be able to touch the harmonic point with your index finger.

If fingerpicking, you could try using the thumb to pick and the index finger to touch the harmonic point.

Using the ring finger to pluck and index to touch the harmonic resembles a classical right hand position.

Playing fretted harmonics requires a nifty right hand technique. You have to pluck the string with one digit while simultaneously touching the string at its harmonic point with another.

Pinched harmonics

This plectrum technique has been used by Billy Gibbons on some of ZZ Top's biggest hits. It adds pizzazz to solos and is often used with string bends.

To try out pinched harmonics, it helps to have the plectrum quite deep in your grip (i.e. with very little tip showing). Immediately after striking the string at a slight angle, touch it very lightly with the thumb or plectrum and forefinger. This has to occur in one small movement, as if you are giving the string a slight pinch. The note still rings, but the extra touch brings out harmonics that add a high-pitched squeal.

Try to catch the string lightly as soon as it is picked.

Double hammer-ons and pull-offs

Whole chords can be hammered-on or pulled-off at the same time, but just two strings at once is more common. This technique is often used when playing patterns that have notes at the same fret on adjoining strings – as used in the pentatonic improvisation. Multiple pull-offs and hammer-ons can be played with any two left hand fingers moved together – the 1st and 2nd, or 2nd and 3rd, or even the 3rd and 4th fingers together at the higher fret positions.

Flurries of double hammer-ons and pull-offs are a characteristic of Jimi Hendrix's playing style.

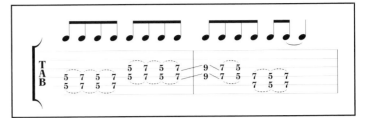

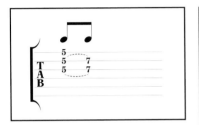

A common double hammer lick on the B and G strings at fret 5.

A Bluesy sequence of double hammers and pulls in A. The two bars are linked by a two-string slide. Practise hammering-on and pulling-off these together from the 5th to 7th fret.

Tapping techniques

Tapping is the art of using both hands to play hammered-on and pulled-off notes. Simple tapping uses hammer-ons either with the plectrum or with one or two fingers of the right hand. It provides extra notes at a greater speed and with larger leaps in pitch than the left hand alone could manage. Tapping requires shorter nails on the right hand than you would require for picking. The common lick, shown here, uses a rolling left hand hammer-on (l), with additional high notes provided by tapping (or hammering-on) using the right (r).

Tapping is facilitated by the super-fast action of modern electric guitars, which allows a player to sound as many notes as they have fingers. Solo guitarists can use tapping to accompany themselves – hammering chords and bass notes with one hand while playing melodies with the other. With practice, the right hand can develop all the fretting ability and strength of the left, allowing almost limitless possibilities. Stanley Jordan, Yngwie Malmsteen, Steve Vai and Joe Satriani are all accomplished proponents of the art.

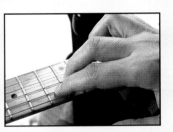

Partial or even whole chords can be tapped with both hands.

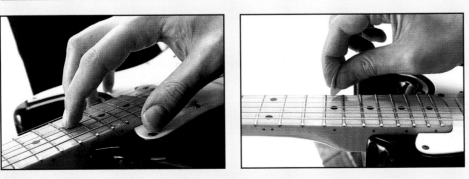

Simple hammer-on tapping, such as in this example of a right hand tap at fret 17, can be performed with a right hand finger – usually the index finger (left) – or with a plectrum (right). The edge of the plectrum has to be brought down hard onto the string for it to sound clearly. Kirk Hammet of Metallica uses the latter technique rapidly and repeatedly to create flurries of high notes over a solo.

NOTE NAMES, FLATS AND SHARPS

An indispensable reference to the names of all the notes on the guitar up to the 12th fret.

You will have noticed by now that all notes on the guitar are named by the first seven letters of the alphabet, from A through to G, with the occasional addition of 'sharps' or 'flats'. Here's a closer look at how this system works.

The notes run from A, B, C, D, E, F, G, and back to A again. The distance between one A and the next is an octave, from the Latin for 'eighth', as in the eighth letter (see page 41).

Semitones and tones

On a guitar's fretboard, the difference between one fretted note and the next as you travel up any one string is equivalent to a semitone. A difference of two frets, or two semitones, equals a tone.

Sharps and flats

There are notes that occur between A and B, C and D, D and E, F and G, and G and A that are called flats or sharps. You will notice that not all note names have sharps or flats. When a note is called a sharp, it means that it is a semitone, or a fret, above its letter note, while a flat indicates that it is a semitone, or a fret, below.

A sharp and B flat are the same note; sharp literally means one fret up from A, while flat means one fret down from B, respectively. Both lead you to the same places: either fret 1 on the A string, fret 3 on the G string or fret 6 on the top or bottom E string.

Previously we only used one name for each sharp or flat note, because guitarists tend to use one term more than another; you will rarely hear a player talk about A

Why there are flats and sharps

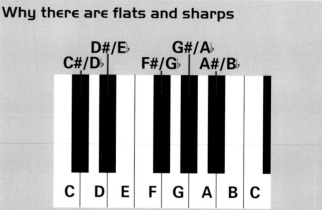

The note naming system evolved around a keyboard rather than a guitar. Between C and D on a keyboard there is a black key, which is C sharp. As a black key, it's clearly different – and so, for a keyboard player, having it called a sharp or a flat is useful. Also, on a standard notation stave, there is a line, or a space between two lines, for each letter note. The sharps or flats are either written as symbols (# for sharp and ♭ for flat) alongside each note when they occur, or are indicated in a 'key signature' at the beginning of a piece; this tells you exactly which notes should be flattened or sharpened throughout. The great advantage of TAB, of course, is that it doesn't need to use flat or sharp symbols, as every note is shown by the fret number on each string.

sharp or G flat, even though sometimes it might be strictly correct. We have, for example, frequently used F sharp, but never called it G flat.

The diagram below shows the name of every note on each string, up to the 12th fret, after which the pattern repeats an octave higher. Both flat and sharp names are shown, with the least commonly used in brackets.

	Fret 1	Fret 2	Fret 3	Fret 4	Fret 5	Fret 6	Fret 7	Fret 8	Fret 9	Fret 10	Fret 11	Fret 12
E	F	F♯ (G♭)	G	G♯ (A♭)	A	(A♯) B♭	B	C	C♯ (D♭)	D	(D♯) E♭	E
B	C	C♯ (D♭)	D	(D♯) E♭	E	F	F♯ (G♭)	G	G♯ (A♭)	A	(A♯) B♭	B
G	G♯ (A♭)	A	(A♯) B♭	B	C	C♯ (D♭)	D	(D♯) E♭	E	F	F♯ (G♭)	G
D	(D♯) E♭	E	F	F♯ (G♭)	G	G♯ (A♭)	A	(A♯) B♭	B	C	C♯ (D♭)	D
A	(A♯) B♭	B	C	C♯ (D♭)	D	(D♯) E♭	E	F	F♯ (G♭)	G	G♯ (A♭)	A
E	F	F♯ (G♭)	G	G♯ (A♭)	A	(A♯) B♭	B	C	C♯ (D♭)	D	(D♯) E♭	E

CHORD GLOSSARY

This feature brings you many of the standard, as well as a few of the more unusual, chord shapes to get your fingers around and learn by heart.

We have brought together chords found in five commonly used keys (three major and two minor) as an invaluable, at-a-glance reference source. The six main chords for the major keys of D, G, and E follow the sequence of I, II, IV, V, V7 and VI (the relative minor).

Each group of six chords, for both the major and the minor keys, is supplemented by three extra patterns. These can be used to add splashes of more exotic harmony to the sound of the standard chords. We have tried to incorporate as wide a variety of optional chords as possible, including augmented, suspended, minor 7th and diminished chords, as well as other, more complex-sounding ones. Some of these should be familiar to you; others – for example, Bm7♭5 – you will not have come across in this book.

Try strumming around the six main chords in each key, until you are used to their fingering, the movements required to change smoothly between them, their sound and their relationship to each other. Once you are comfortable with them, start to add some of the additional chords between the standard ones.

These pages show only the 1st or 2nd position shapes for all the chords, with a couple of exceptions – Gaug, for example, is played in 3rd position. However, feel free to substitute any of the shapes with their barre chord or higher-position equivalents. For example, working out how to play the six main chords given for the key of D around 5th position using barred A and E shapes would be a very useful exercise in itself.

Minor key chords

The six main chords given for the key of E minor and A minor aren't in the same sequence as those for the three major keys. Instead, we have simply shown the chords that are commonly played in these keys. Again, both sets of six are followed by three optional chords that will add extra flavour to any minor sequence.

Chords in the key of D

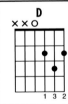

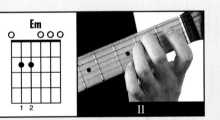

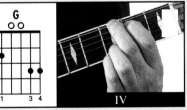

The key note chord, D major.

The familiar, two-finger shape of an E minor chord.

The four-finger G chord shape.

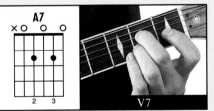

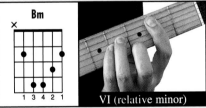

The standard three-finger A shape.

A7 is often followed by a return to the D major key chord.

B minor is often played as an A minor shape barred at the 2nd fret.

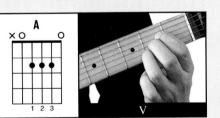

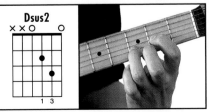

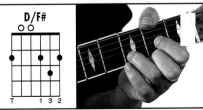

Dmaj7 can be played with a barre across the top three strings at fret 2.

Dsus2 has an open top E string.

D with an F# bass note, which is fretted here by the thumb.

Chords in the key of G

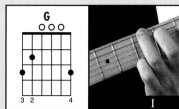
G

This G chord fingering works well with C major shifts.

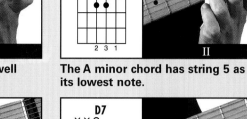
Am

The A minor chord has string 5 as its lowest note.

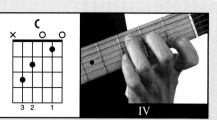
C

C major is a common partner to G in this key.

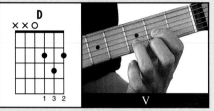
D

The D major chord with its familiar triangular finger pattern.

D7

For D7, finger 1 at fret 1 on the B string provides the 7th note – C.

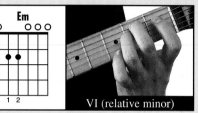
Em

E minor with finger 2 in the same place as for G major, above.

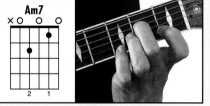
Ddim

Used sparingly, diminished chords spice up a song.

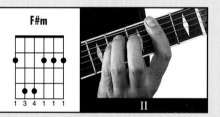
Am7

An open G turns A minor into A minor 7.

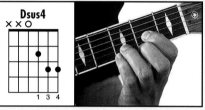
Dsus4

Dsus4 is a familiar suspended chord, often paired with a pure D major.

Chords in the key of E

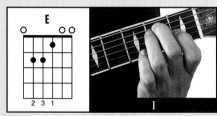
E

A standard 1st position E chord.

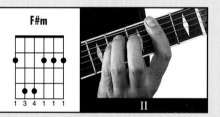
F#m

F#m played as a barre chord shape in 2nd position.

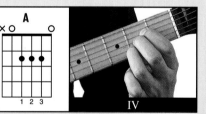
A

A major is referred to as the subdominant chord in the key of E.

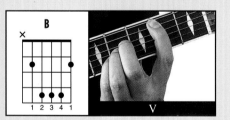
B

B major is played with a five-string finger barre.

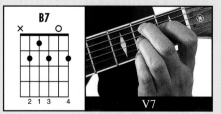
B7

A useful 1st position version of B7.

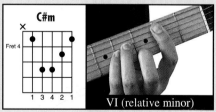
C#m

C#m is played as a barred A minor shape in 4th position.

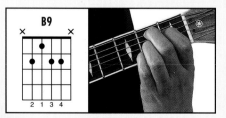
B9

A rich, jazzy-sounding chord. The 9th note is fretted by the 4th finger.

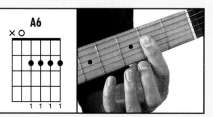
A6

A6 can be played with a barre across the top 4 strings at fret 2.

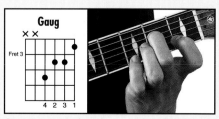
Gaug

Augmented chords, such as Gaug, are often found in 'Fifties rock'n'roll.

Chords in the key of A minor

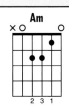

Am

A minor has a powerful, melancholy effect.

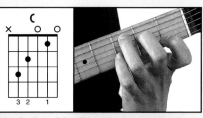

C

This C chord is the relative major in the key of A minor.

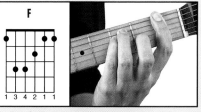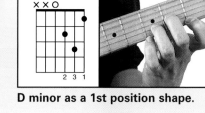

Dm

D minor as a 1st position shape.

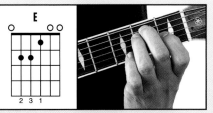

E

E major shares its left hand shape with the key chord.

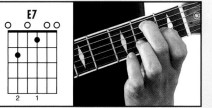

E7

E7 – lifting finger 3 from E major provides the 7th note.

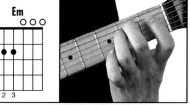

F

F – the full six-string barre chord in 1st position is shown here.

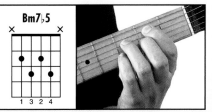

Bm7♭5

Bm7♭5 – an exotic-sounding chord with a flattened 5th on the D string.

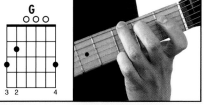

G

Am, G, F then E is a classic chord sequence.

Em

The E minor chord can be used with A minor to heighten a sad mood.

Chords in the key of E minor

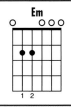

Em

The E minor chord takes full advantage of the open strings.

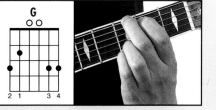

G

G major with finger 1 in the same place as in the key chord.

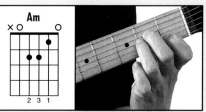

Am

A minor is a straightforward shift from E minor.

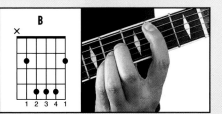

B

B major is the important dominant chord in E minor.

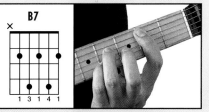

B7

The B7 chord, this time using the 2nd position shape.

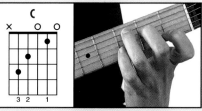

C

C major works well in alternation with the key chord.

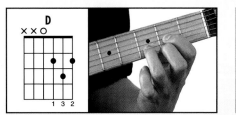

D

D major is often played after E minor.

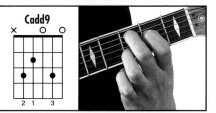

Cadd9

Cadd9 is a rich, full-sounding chord.

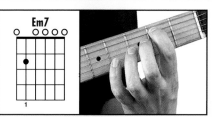

Em7

Em7 adds the subtle colouring of an open D to E minor.

111

ELECTRIC BASS GUITARS

A look at the history and development of the modern electric bass, and a guide to some classic models.

Bass guitars are a hybrid creation. In the 'Forties, Leo Fender noticed that double bass players were being drowned out in increasingly amplified bands. To overcome this, some players were fitting pick-ups to their acoustic double basses, while others were playing Stratocasters with the bottom strings de-tuned an octave lower than the original. In making his electric bass, Fender stuck to the basic guitar design and tuning so that guitarists could double up as bassists. In 1951, the Fender bass was born.

Stronger instruments

The basic elements of an electric bass guitar are the same as a six-string. However, the extra stress caused by the heavy strings and long scale length means that the bridge, the tuning machines and the neck have to be chunkier and stronger than they would on a six-string. Most guitar manufacturers have their own line of basses, but some, such as Wal or Alembic, specialize in basses only.

An electric bass can be played either with the right hand fingers, a plectrum or with the sophisticated techniques of 'pulling' and 'slapping'. The strings on a bass guitar are tuned, from 4th to 1st, to the notes E, A, D and G – the same as the bottom four strings on a six-string but an octave lower. As a result, any scales or chords that work on the bottom four strings of a six-string will have the same fingering on a bass. Effective bass playing, however, is about economy, and due to the depth of the note and the strength required to play a bass guitar, bassists are more likely to play single notes than chords. If you get a chance to play one, give it a go – you might find that the depth and feel of a bass guitar give it a particular attraction.

Motorhead's Lemmy holds up his Rickenbacker, customized with a steel scratch plate and fittings.

Fender Precision

A straightforward, uncomplicated instrument, the Fender Precision has become the bass of choice for most rock musicians. It has a 'split' single-coil pick-up (split to cover the top two and lower two strings evenly), with four pole pieces in each of the two staggered halves. This results in an even string-to-string tone. It was given the name 'Precision' because, unlike the double bass, it has frets, allowing players to fret notes precisely.
Played by: John Deacon (Queen), Alex James (Blur), Colin Greenwood (Radiohead), Martyn Casey (Nick Cave And The Bad Seeds), Barry Adamson, Paul McGuigan (Oasis) and many others

Fender Jazz

With its slim neck, the Fender Jazz is a delight to play. It has two single-coil pick-ups with individual controls. These can be blended together to create a surprisingly wide variety of tones, from a smooth low sound to a mid-range punchy one.
Played by: Nicky Wire (Manic Street Preachers), Noel Redding (Jimi Hendrix Experience)

Rickenbacker basses

The Rickenbacker 4000 series basses have a very distinctive shape and sound. First made in the late 'Fifties, some models have one output for each of the two pick-ups, which allows a player to create a wall of bass noise. This, combined with a punchy and aggressive tone, makes it a good choice for players who want to stand out in their rhythm section.
Played by: Lemmy (Motorhead), Bruce Foxton (The Jam)

Fender's Noel Redding bass, a deluxe Jazz.

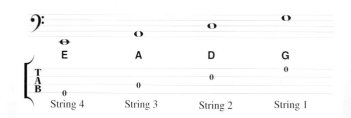

Gibson basses

The first Gibson bass was the EB1. It had a body shaped like a violin, and Hofner's copy of it became famous in the hands of Paul McCartney. Later Gibson models, such as the Thunderbird and the RD series, were sturdier in design.
Played by: John Entwistle (The Who), Paul McCartney

Hi-tech basses – Alembic and Wal

The equivalent of Superstrats, these hi-tech basses have very specialized pick-ups, which give the player a great deal of 'bottom end' response. They also have beautifully made necks with full access to the upper frets. As a result, they are very suitable for the bottom-heavy frequencies beloved of dance, reggae and funk.
Played by: Mark King (Level 42), Jaco Pastorius, Stanley Clarke

Fretless electric basses

A fretless bass resembles a double bass in that it has no frets. This calls for a more accurate left hand technique since the pitch of each note is determined by the exact placement of the left hand fingers. As a result, the notes have less attack and punch, but this allows for a great deal of expression through the left hand fingers. In some players' hands, these basses become lead instruments.
Played by: Sting, Jaco Pastorius, Pino Palladino, Mick Karn (Japan)

Acoustic basses

These are close to their six-string electro-acoustic counterparts, and feature built-in transducer pick-ups to amplify the guitar's 'natural' acoustic sound. They are often used on 'unplugged' sessions by bassists who wish to achieve an acoustic sound without having to master the double bass.

Five-string and headless basses

There are always some players who feel that the normal allocation of strings is insufficient. For these people, there are five-string basses with an extra, deep B string. Fender even made a six-string bass, the Bass VI, but it was discontinued in the 'Seventies. Steinberg patented a short-scale bass with no headstock – the strings are tuned at the bridge.
Played by: Bass VI – Stefan Olsdal (Placebo), Steinberg – Bill Wyman (ex-Rolling Stones)

The notes of a bass guitar's open strings. Notice the bass clef symbol at the left of the notation. Since a bass has only four strings, bass TAB is written on just four lines.

Other manufacturers

There is as wide a variety of basses as there is of six-strings. Aria, Yamaha, Ibanez and Westone are some of the other manufacturers who make very playable and affordable, quality instruments.

Sting in the last days of The Police, playing a fretless bass.

THE SPANISH GUITAR

The materials and processes used in the construction of classical guitars stem from one of the longest and richest traditions.

Many of the best makes of acoustic guitar are manufactured by firms with a long family tradition of craftsmanship. This is especially true of Spanish guitar-makers. The history of the Spanish guitar is full of famous craftsmen proud of their heritage and family names – Ramirez, de Torres and Rodriguez – who continue to produce the finest guitars.

Quality of wood

The density of different woods and the methods by which they are joined together all affect the tone of the instrument. Certain woods are used for their specific tonal and physical properties. The particular cut of the wood – for example, quarter cut or cross cut, so named after the position on a log that they are taken from – is also a consideration as it affects its positional strength. For a quality instrument, the wood has to be seasoned for several years, as this minimizes the risk of warping from changes in temperature and humidity.

THE HEADSTOCK VENEER
The surface of the headstock is usually finished with a decorative veneer (i.e. a very thin layer of wood, which has a colourful and attractive grain). This is purely an aesthetic addition.

THE NECK
The neck is made of mahogany or cedar – strong, resilient woods that are resistant to bending or warping.

THE FRETBOARD (OR FINGERBOARD)
This needs to have an even, flawless surface for the player's fingertips, so it is usually made from a hard, dark wood, such as ebony, mahogany or rosewood – all dense enough to give a satin-smooth finish.

THE SOUNDBOARD
This is the most crucial resonating piece of any acoustic guitar because the bridge is mounted here and therefore all vibrations are transmitted through it. Spruce or cedar are ideal woods for a soundboard – the long, fine grain is excellent for transmitting vibrations, while the wood is sufficiently hard to retain a degree of strength even when cut into thin sections.

THE BODY (THE SIDES AND BACK)
The soundbox body of a good-quality Spanish guitar is often made of rosewood, usually from India or Brazil. This dense but fairly light wood has a rich, attractive grain.

A RODRIGUEZ CLASSICAL GUITAR
This fine guitar clearly demonstrates a typical range of woods and their deployment.

THE BRIDGE
This is made of rosewood or another hard wood from India or Brazil, to transmit all vibrations into the soundboard.

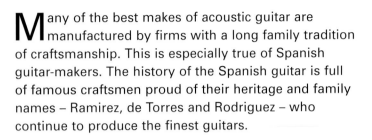

Body construction

The wood for the sides (or ribs) of a Spanish guitar has to be steam-heated into the instrument's distinctive curves. The back of the soundbox is commonly made of two 'book-ended' pieces of wood. These are split from the same section of wood, so each mirrors the other's grain. They are often joined by a decorative cleat. The back is then cross-braced for added strength.

One 'rib' of a Rodriguez guitar being heated into shape.

The back of the Rodriguez, clearly showing the matching 'book-ended' pieces of wood and decorative cleat joining them.

Bracing

Back cross-bracing gives support and strength, but the bracing of the soundboard is more important. Traditional fan-pattern bracing features thin strips of spruce glued to the underside of the soundboard, which radiate down to the base of the guitar from the soundhole. These ensure the maximum transmission of vibrations across the surface of the soundboard from the bridge. Other bracing patterns have different acoustic properties.

Careful assembly

The back, sides and soundboard are joined together with a 'kerfed' lining – a strip of strong wood, slotted for flexibility, which curves to match the contours of the sides. Cheap makes will cut costs on the bracing and lining materials, while better manufacturers will use good-quality woods. The neck is slotted into place. The bottom of the soundbox is given added strength with an end block that secures all parts together. The heel of the guitar – the back of the neck at the point where it meets the soundbox – is built up with layers of laminated wood, and is finished with a final layer called the 'toe'. The bridge of the guitar is carefully glued into position on the soundboard surface. Lastly, the fretboard is glued into place along the neck and over the body join.

Finishing touches

Once a guitar has been completed, expert luthiers (such as the American John Gilbert) will test the acoustic properties of different areas, using everything from the naked ear to transducer pick-ups. The guitar will then receive a great deal of further finishing treatment – frets will be sanded until smooth and even at every point, and as much time might be spent on creating a beautiful varnish finish on a Spanish guitar as it takes to build one.

Flamenco guitars

Guitars intended for Flamenco playing – essentially a folk style without the courtly status of the classical instrument – are usually made from a lighter wood, such as cypress. Flamenco guitars have a thinner soundboard, lower action and lighter construction, resulting in a warmer tone with attack. A renowned Flamenco (as well as classical) guitar-maker is Domingo Esteso.

Construction of steel-string guitars

The materials and construction of steel-strung acoustics are essentially the same as for Spanish guitars, but with more emphasis on strength. The struts across the back are of greater thickness, the soundboard braces are more numerous and the neck usually has a truss rod. Along with adjustable bridges for accurate intonation and high precision machine heads, these once distinctly steel-strung features have been incorporated into many modern makes of Spanish guitar, such as the Rodriguez shown here. Many recent brands use parallel strutting and sophisticated internal bracing, both of which add to the guitar's sound projection.

Although it lacks a soundhole, this soundboard from an Ovation Adamas electro-acoustic shows a fan-shaped pattern of bracing.

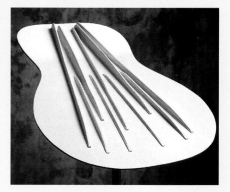

FROM RAGS TO RICHES

Charting the rise and rise of the 12-string guitar.

You play a 12-string guitar in exactly the same way as a six-string. The extra strings that double-up with the standard ones are either an octave above (as in the bottom E, A, D and G strings), or double-up the same note (as in the B and top E strings – strings that could be tuned to an octave above these two would have to be impracticably thin). The paired strings are set close enough to be fretted simultaneously by the same finger without requiring any new technique.

Drawbacks

The paired strings have to be tuned to each other as well as to the other strings. This means that tuning a 12-string takes more time and patience than required to tune a six-string. The extra resistance caused by having two strings in the place of one does limit left hand techniques, especially bends. Structurally speaking, a 12-string has to have extra bracing and be built to withstand the extra strain. Also, having a total of 12 tuning machines results in an odd-looking extended headstock.

Advantages

By their nature, acoustic 12-strings have more volume, and chords played on them have a rich range of octaves. Both these attributes make 12-strings great for loud strumming. Fingerpicking styles also sound particularly strong, and arpeggios leap out – the double strings enhancing figures that would sound weaker on a six-string.

Acoustic 12-strings

One theory about the origins of the 12-string at the turn of the century in the USA is that the main luthiers, in New York and Chicago, were of Italian descent and were reworking the double-course (double-string) styles of

A close-up of an Ovation 12-string, showing the sequence of octave and standard strings.

classical Italian instruments such as the mandolin. Another theory is that the 12-string is Mexican in origin. Latin America has many double-course variants of the standard six-string guitar – such as the *tiple*, the *charango* and the *cuatro* – and Mexico has a large number of guitar variants, from the diminutive *guitarra de golpe* to the massive *guitarron*.

The 12-string guitar was initially considered a crude relative of the six-string, and was ignored by prestigious makers such as Martin and Gibson. Since cheaper manufacturers often built 12-strings, their buyers tended to be relatively poor. However, for busking or performing musicians, in an age before amplification, the extra volume of a 12-string was an asset.

Three players are particularly associated with the 12-string acoustic. One was Lydia Mendoza, known as *La Cancionista de los Pobres* (The Poor People's Songstress), a Mexican-born star for the rural poor, who continued to perform until retiring in the 'Eighties. Another was Blind Willie McTell, who exploited the range of the 12-string with a complex, driving bass style of fingerpicking. Finally, there was the king of the 12-string, Blues legend Huddie Leadbetter, better known as Leadbelly. Both McTell and Leadbelly played a Stella 12-string, which is a large, loud guitar. Championed by folk archivists Alan and John Lomax, Leadbelly had a huge influence on the development of folk and rock music. (Nirvana covered Leadbelly's *In The Pines* as the climax of their *MTV Unplugged* concert.) Folk singer Pete Seeger, who describes the sound of a 12-string as 'the clanging of the bells', took his cue from Leadbelly and used the power of the 12-string to play his protest songs at crowded venues in the 'Fifties and 'Sixties. Players such as Leo Kottke stuck with the instrument through the following decades, ensuring it would remain a viable concern.

With the 'Sixties folk boom, manufacturers woke up to the 12-string market. Guild, Gibson, Bozo, Martin, Epiphone and Washburn now all produce popular models. Ovation's strident 12-strings are a common sight with rock and country acts.

Joan Armatrading with an Ovation Legend 12-string.

Electric models

The real boom in the popularity of 12-strings came in the 'Sixties, thanks to two players in particular – George Harrison of The Beatles and Jim (later Roger) McGuinn of The Byrds.

Inspired by the folk boom, the American guitar company Rickenbacker decided to produce a 12-string version of their already popular 300 series. The characteristic bright, ringing Rickenbacker tone, ideal for arpeggios and suspended chords, lent itself to a 12-string set-up. In an ingenious alteration to standard acoustic 12-string design, they removed the need for an extended headstock for the extra six tuning machines by setting them at 90 degrees to the rest, like the tuning machines of Spanish guitars. This left just the standard six in the usual position, making tuning much less confusing. The usual order of the paired strings – octave string then normal – was also reversed.

The Beatles were the world's most famous Rickenbacker users, so Harrison was given the new 12-string version of the 360 model. Its ringing sound embellished *You Can't Do That*, *Eight Days A Week* and *A Hard Day's Night*, to name just three. The sales of 12-strings soared. One convert

A Rickenbacker 360 12-string.

was Jim McGuinn, lead guitarist of The Byrds, who bought a Rickenbacker 12-string after seeing The Beatles film *A Hard Day's Night*. The jangling arpeggios McGuinn played on it were aptly described by The Byrds hit single *Turn! Turn! Turn!*, a version of a Pete Seeger song. The chiming tones of the 12-string became a defining sound of psychedelia, inextricably bound up with protest and change. Tom Petty, Johnny Marr and REM's Peter Buck are guitarists who have since mined the rich seam offered by the Rickenbacker 12-string.

Rickenbacker is by no means the only company to make 12-string electrics; Fender and Gibson have many excellent 12-string models. Led Zeppelin's Jimmy Page used the richness of Gibson 12-strings, heard to great effect on the band's classic *Stairway To Heaven*.

Jim McGuinn of The Byrds, playing his three pick-up Rickenbacker 370 12-string.

GOLDS, SUNBURSTS AND REISSUES

The history and specifications of one of the most revered of solid-bodied electric guitars.

Like any successful guitar, the Les Paul has spawned a host of imitations and direct copies. Good Les Pauls are often said to 'play themselves' – a comment on their easy action. The action, wide frets and consistent intonation mean that the instrument lends itself to solos and string bends, and the simplicity of its design and quality of manufacture make it a very reliable guitar for stage use. However, the rich, high-output sound and considerable weight of the guitar are not to every player's tastes.

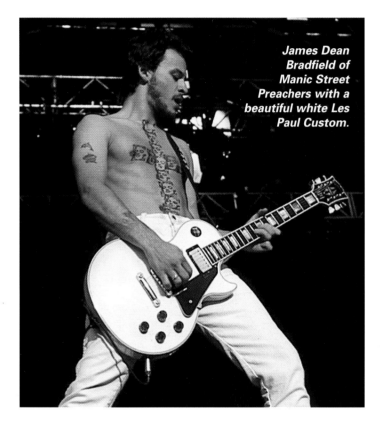

James Dean Bradfield of Manic Street Preachers with a beautiful white Les Paul Custom.

Log jam

Under the guidance of jazz guitarist and innovator Les Paul, the Gibson company began investigating the potential of solid-body electric guitars in the early 1930s. Envisioning a solid-body guitar with very long, natural sustain, Les Paul built a prototype electric called 'the Log', but it was not taken too seriously by Gibson. However, the success of Fender's Broadcaster (an early form of the Telecaster) made the company think again. Gibson craftsman Ted McCarty began to experiment with the acoustic properties of various woods for the guitar's body. He found that mahogany had an appealingly warm tone, with a broad harmonic spectrum, and that maple had exceptional sustaining properties.

The Les Paul Standard

Under Les Paul's supervision, around 50 prototype guitars were built. The final version was a beautifully made, heavy guitar with an easy action, remarkably rich sound and very long, natural sustain. However, the Gibson company nearly removed their name from the guitar as they feared it would be a flop. They couldn't have been more wrong. This first version of the Gibson Les Paul Standard went into production in 1952. It had a solid mahogany body with a laminated half-inch maple 'cap', or surface layer, to maximize the guitar's natural sustain. The pick-ups were a pair of single-coil P-90 'soapbars', each with their own volume and tone control with a distinctive 'hatbox'-style knob. As well as high-quality Grover machine heads, the strings ended in a trapeze tailpiece and the frets were fatter in cross-section than those of their close rivals, Fender. The contoured, single-cutaway body resembled a smaller version of an arch-top semi-acoustic, but the full swelling curvature of the top and the stunning golden finish set it a world apart.

Lasting refinements

Up until 1960, Gibson issued several refinements of this initial model, as well as a similar guitar called the Les Paul Custom. The 1957 'black beauty' version of the Custom had three pick-ups and such a remarkably easy action that it was nicknamed 'the fretless wonder'. The first, most important and enduring refinement made to the original Les Paul was the 'tun-o-matic' bridge, which consisted of a separate bridge and tailpiece, the former with individual saddles for accurate and easily adjustable intonation (see page 65). The next important addition was the introduction of humbucker pick-ups. The 'Patent Applied For' (or PAF) pick-ups, now highly sought after, enhanced the instrument's already considerable sustain (see page 66-67). Both these additions became standard features on all Les Pauls.

Sunburst

In 1958, Gibson made one more change to the classic Les Paul Standard. They discontinued the traditional gold finish and introduced a new 'cherry sunburst' effect – a warm, luxurious look achieved by a careful combination of wood stains and lacquers. Sunburst Les Pauls are among the most highly prized of all solid-body electric guitars.

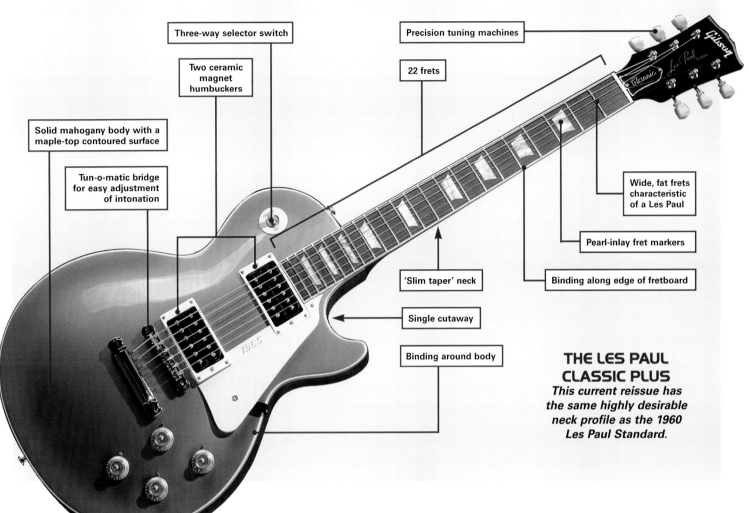

Three-way selector switch

Two ceramic magnet humbuckers

Solid mahogany body with a maple-top contoured surface

Tun-o-matic bridge for easy adjustment of intonation

Precision tuning machines

22 frets

Wide, fat frets characteristic of a Les Paul

Pearl-inlay fret markers

'Slim taper' neck

Binding along edge of fretboard

Single cutaway

Binding around body

THE LES PAUL CLASSIC PLUS
This current reissue has the same highly desirable neck profile as the 1960 Les Paul Standard.

Rediscovered classics

During the late 'Fifties, Les Pauls faced fierce competition and didn't sell very well. Gibson began to alter the basic design, introducing double cutaways on Les Paul Specials and Juniors. Finally, in 1960, they discontinued the old-style Les Pauls altogether. The new style had the sharp horns of the Gibson SG (Solid Guitar), and Les Paul's name was eventually removed from the guitar's title. Across the Atlantic, however, the heroes of the British Blues boom and the subsequent 'British invasion', including players such as Jimmy Page and Eric Clapton, were treating Les Pauls with an almost holy reverence. This caused a renewed interest in the original Les Pauls, and rock

The Jimmy Page Signature Les Paul Standard, with push/pull controls and other refinements.

musicians started to pay thousands of pounds for vintage models. Les Paul was reunited with Gibson, and the company began manufacturing Les Pauls again in the late 'Sixties, with several new variants on the original theme. In the 'Seventies, the rise of heavy rock, the emergence of the guitar hero and the ascendancy of the supergroup ensured that the Les Paul became the desired guitar for any aspiring 'axe hero' and a status symbol in its own right.

Reissues

There was some fluctuation in quality in the following decades, but in the 'Nineties, Gibson took great pains to reissue classic models from every period with the specifications and quality of workmanship of the originals. Among the many players who've become synonymous with the Les Paul, a few stand out, not least Jimmy Page, who, in his Led Zeppelin heyday, was almost always seen sporting a beautiful sunburst Les Paul. Now his signature model is available commercially, built with Page's specified settings and features.

STRAT FACTS

The development of the 'Fifties guitar that has been the choice of legends for four decades.

As the Fender company's single most successful model, the history of the Strat is closely linked with the history of the company itself. Its founder, Leo Fender, was a radio repairman who began making amplifiers and instruments at the end of World War II. By the early 'Fifties, his guitars had become popular with the western swing, country and rhythm Blues players who laid the foundations for rock'n'roll. Fender's best-selling model was the Telecaster (originally called the Broadcaster), which was a workman-like guitar, simple in design and sound, and was fitted with a bolt-on neck to simplify the construction process.

Fender firsts

In response to demands for a more comfortable guitar, Leo Fender decided to build a new model with many innovative features that would make it a market leader. The guitar would be packed with unique additions – the 'Fender firsts'.

He built a new body with double cutaways, which gave better access to the higher frets and reduced the guitar's weight. A further refinement was to contour the body back and front. The contouring on the back allows the instrument to sit on a player's hips without cutting into his or her ribs, while the front contouring makes for easier right-hand movement.

With three pick-ups in place of the usual two, Fender's new guitar also featured a new tremolo system. The distinctive curly headstock was devised to keep the section of string above the top nut in line with the ringing string, thereby minimizing friction. In a final improvement on the Telecaster, the Strat was given a bridge with

The Fender Strat has a continuing appeal. Steve Malkmus of Pavement uses this Strat as his main guitar.

individually adjustable saddles for accurate intonation. The result was a highly versatile, good-looking and playable instrument.

Hidden extras

The original model had a three-way selector switch. This gave the player the choice of which pick-up to use – from the biting, glassy treble of the bridge pick-up to the distinctive, 'round' sound of the neck pick-up. But players soon discovered a further set of options. The Strat's pick-up switch could be left in-between the three intended settings, giving an 'out-of-phase' combination of any two pick-ups. The result was a peculiar, 'hollow', nasal tone, with real bite and cut. Fender incorporated these extra options into the five-way switch now fitted as standard. Eric Clapton and Mark Knopfler are two players who make full use of the twangy sound of a Strat's intermediate 2nd and 4th switch positions.

Trems and teens

Leo Fender's business partner, Don Randall, dubbed the model the 'Stratocaster', a name designed to sound futuristic and space-age. This new gizmo-packed guitar went into production in 1954, but was initially regarded by many as a trendy toy for teenagers. However, serious guitarists soon warmed to the comfort and ease of playing offered by the Strat, and it quickly became the instrument of choice for the leading figures of rock'n'roll. Buddy Holly's ringing chords were played on a Strat. In the UK, Hank Marvin was the first player really to exploit the Strat's ringing lead tone and tremolo, while in the USA, Dick Dale used the Strat's treble sting in his frenetic surf guitar-style (typified by his version of *Miserlou* on the *Pulp Fiction* soundtrack). However, the man who did more to popularize the Strat than any other has to be Jimi Hendrix. As the most imitated and

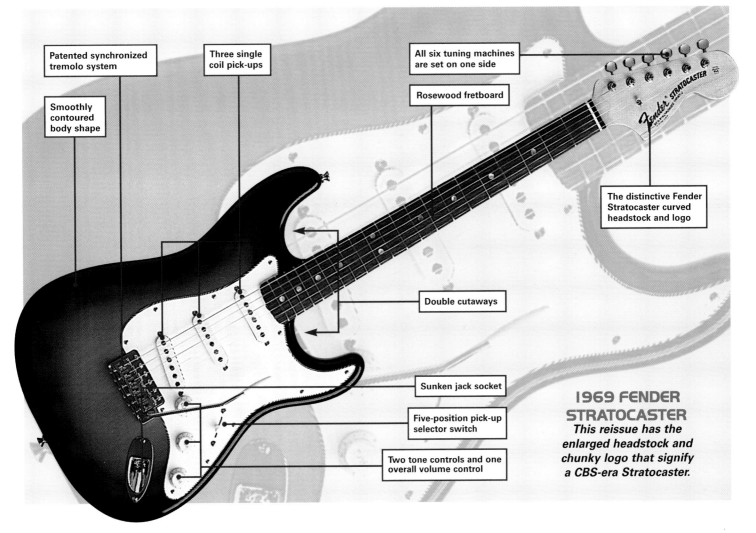

Patented synchronized tremolo system

Three single coil pick-ups

All six tuning machines are set on one side

Smoothly contoured body shape

Rosewood fretboard

The distinctive Fender Stratocaster curved headstock and logo

Double cutaways

Sunken jack socket

Five-position pick-up selector switch

Two tone controls and one overall volume control

1969 FENDER STRATOCASTER
This reissue has the enlarged headstock and chunky logo that signify a CBS-era Stratocaster.

venerated guitarist of the 20th century, it was inevitable that people should want to own the guitar that Hendrix tested to the limit.

CBS 'Seventies

In the 'Fifties, Leo Fender contracted a streptococcal infection, which troubled him for a decade. In 1965, convinced that he didn't have long to live, he sold the company to CBS. But shortly afterwards, he recovered and returned to CBS/Fender to continue producing guitars. However, standards of manufacturing are generally acknowledged to have slipped after the sell-out, and pre-CBS models have become highly sought after.

'Seventies Strats had a larger headstock than their predecessors, and an altered logo. Originally, 'Fender Stratocaster' was written on the headstock in spaghetti-thin type. Then, from 1964 onwards, it came in a modern, more

Two current luxury production models: the Jerry Donahue (above) and Eric Clapton (below) signature Strats.

substantial-looking gold version. On CBS-era guitars, however, the legend appears in thick black type. Current models have reverted to a version of the 1964 logo.

One innovation found on 'Seventies models is the 'micro tilt' neck which allowed for fine adjustment of the neck angle at the join.

Vintage and state-of-the-art

Under new ownership, Fender underwent a revival in the 'Eighties. The company capitalized on the Strat's status by sanctioning both a Korean-built budget version (the Squier series) and the manufacture of Strats abroad under license. In descending order of quality, American-made Strats have alder or ash bodies like the originals, Mexican-built ones tend to have poplar bodies, while Japanese-built Strats are usually made of basswood and are essentially budget models.

Nearly all Strat necks are made of maple, a dense blond wood. The fretboard is constructed using either the maple of the neck (but given a high gloss varnish) or a separate piece of rosewood that is left 'unfinished'. There are many refinements on Strats to suit every taste, from Lace Sensor pick-ups to locking top nuts.

121

THE LEGENDARY MARTIN Ds

The development of the big-bodied acoustic that transformed the shape and sound of the flat-top steel string.

The Martin Guitar Company has been producing acoustic instruments for over 150 years and is a byword for excellence in craftsmanship. Whereas its equivalent or rival companies, such as Gibson, would have to concede that there have been fluctuations in quality over the years – owing to changes of factories or management – Martin can honestly and uniquely claim to have made instruments of the highest standards of craftsmanship since 1833.

Family history

One reason for the company's consistent pedigree is a strong family lineage. The company was founded by the man whose initials still grace the headstocks of its guitars, Christian Frederick Martin. Born in Germany in 1796, he learned his trade with the renowned luthier Johann Stauffer in Vienna. Having emigrated to America, Martin opened an instrument workshop and music store in New York, before moving to the more peaceful locale of Nazareth, Pennsylvania, which is where the company remains to this day.

The guitars that C.F. Martin began producing look bizarre by today's standards, with very narrow bodies and all the tuning machines on one side of the headstock. This design, which was heavily influenced by Stauffer, typified the classical guitar shape, until the Spanish guitar blueprint was adopted as standard at the end of the 19th century.

Under the guidance of C.F.'s grandson, Frank Henry Martin, the company greatly extended its product range in the 1920s to cater for the boom in folk and country and western music. Initially, the company just strengthened their gut-string models to accommodate the steel strings favoured by these styles, but the introduction of a belly-shaped bridge, truss rods and a different style of soundboard bracing soon created a whole new species of instrument.

Launch of the Dreadnoughts

The most popular type of Martin guitar has to be the Dreadnought, or D, series. Introduced in 1931, this series was named after the massive British battleship HMS *Dreadnought*. It was a reference to the greater size and strength of the guitars in comparison to earlier models – attributes that were initially frowned upon. Deeper and longer than standard flat-top or classical guitars, the Ds' most noticeable difference was the width of the soundbox – one and a half inches greater at its widest point. This increased the projection of bass frequencies, in contrast with the clear treble and overall balance of smaller 'standard size' instruments.

The company had already made a series of large guitars, with characteristically sloping shoulders and wide waists, for another company called Ditson. When Ditson folded in the 1920s, it left an unexpected demand for these larger instruments. Martin modified the Ditson model and adapted a new style of bracing – known as 'X bracing' – for the soundboard.

The first Martin Dreadnoughts, the D-28 and D-18, were adaptations of existing styles. The HD-28 ('Herringbone Dreadnought') had a fine herringbone pattern around its edging, which added cosmetic appeal to this beautiful-sounding instrument.

Another famous Martin model is the D-45, originally introduced as a special custom-order guitar for singer and country star Gene Autry in 1933. When it went into production on a larger scale, the company modified the

Johnny Cash, country music's Man in Black, with his trusty Martin D-45. Note the name tag to avoid backstage mix-ups with other artists' D-45s.

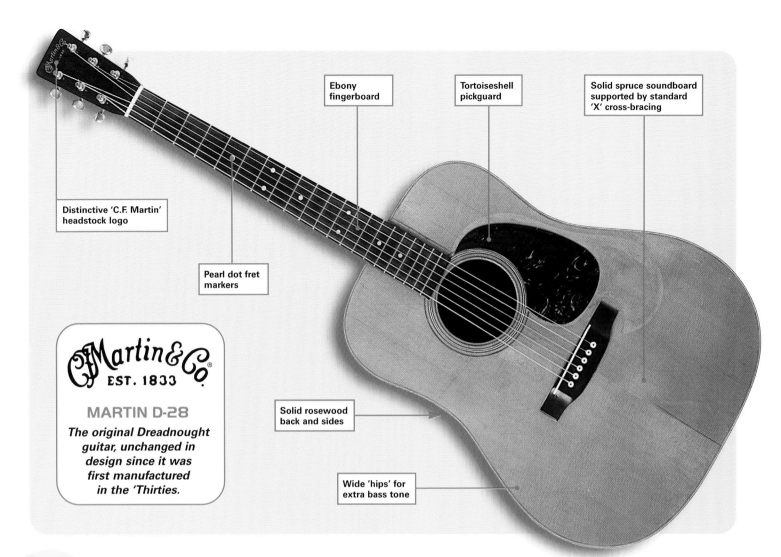

Distinctive 'C.F. Martin'
headstock logo

Pearl dot fret
markers

Ebony
fingerboard

Tortoiseshell
pickguard

Solid spruce soundboard
supported by standard
'X' cross-bracing

Solid rosewood
back and sides

Wide 'hips' for
extra bass tone

MARTIN D-28

The original Dreadnought guitar, unchanged in design since it was first manufactured in the 'Thirties.

neck, having the 14th fret as the one that meets the body, in response to demands from banjo players, who were used to playing on longer necks. However, the original models with the longer soundbox that began at the 12th fret sounded better, so in 1968 Martin reintroduced the legendary D-45S range with the longer soundbox. Vintage D-45s, which have beautiful abalone (mother-of-pearl) inlays, and HD-28s are among the most coveted of all acoustic guitars.

The popularity of Martin's D series spurred the rival Gibson company into producing even larger guitars for their Jumbo, or J, series. These days, all the major manufacturers produce models that copy the dimensions of a Dreadnought.

Vintage value, modern models
Because of the value of Martins, many players refrain from exposing these precious guitars to the hazards of a live stage, preferring to use them in the studio, where the luxurious tone can be fully appreciated without risk. Innumerable players, from Elvis Presley to Richard Thompson, and from Johnny Marr to

Johnny Cash, swear by the perfect sound of a Martin. The sheer quality of craftsmanship and materials means that Martins can fetch astronomical prices, regardless of age. However, the view that Martins are like Rolls-Royces – aspirational luxury items beyond the reach of most players, which you might occasionally hire but could never actually afford to own – is no longer true. As well as a wide range that includes the Jumbo, Auditorium, Orchestra and Classical models, Martin now manufacture the X series, the nearest the company get to a budget range, which is made with all the hand-crafted quality associated with the Martin name. Unlike most other manufacturers, Martin also make left-handed versions of all their models at no extra charge.

Two Dreadnought guitars from Martin's current X range – quality at a reasonable price.

TELE APPEAL

Charting the history of an instantly recognizable guitar that has been around for over 50 years.

Inspired by the success of his solid body steel guitar in the 'Forties, Leo Fender started working on a new instrument. He wanted to design an electric guitar that had a sound as clear as that of a Hawaiian guitar but with none of the feedback problems associated with the vibrating soundboard of an acoustic or archtop guitar. The result was the Broadcaster, a guitar whose guiding principle was practicality rather than aesthetic beauty. Many of its features are now standard, but were originally introduced to facilitate mass production and make repair work easier.

The guitar had minimal contouring and body shaping, with just one cutaway to the right of the neck. Despite being, essentially, a lump of solid wood with a neck bolted on, the Broadcaster was very playable. Guitarists took to it readily, and it became the first mass-produced electric guitar. Its main aesthetic feature was the maple neck, as blonde guitars were popular at the time. Fender chose ash as the wood for guitar bodies with a natural wood finish, and alder for those with a paint finish.

Design quirks

The Broadcaster featured a few innovations. The headstock had all six tuning machines on one side, which avoided fanning the strings above the headstock. The two single coil pick-ups were wired through a three-way selector switch, giving a deep, chunky sound. The bridge and bridge pick-up were set in a tin 'bucket' that added to the springy brightness of the lead pick-up setting. The bridge had only three adjustable saddles, one for each pair of strings. Both were covered by a clip-on cover-plate that players often referred to as the 'ashtray'. The strings passed through holes in the rear of the body before passing up over the bridge, which helped to increase the sustain.

A Telecaster is an essential part of Chrissie Hynde's image.

Hello Tele, bye bye Broad

The Broadcaster went into production in the late 'Forties. However, rival manufacturer Gretsch was having great success with a drum kit of the same name, so Leo Fender picked a new name and re-launched the guitar as the Telecaster, now known to many players as the Tele. This model has remained in production ever since.

Although the design has remained essentially the same, Fender have tried a few variations on the Telecaster theme, including the Esquire, which had only one pick-up, plus the Telecaster Thinline, Deluxe and Custom models, all of which had a more curvaceous scratchplate and Humbucker pick-ups.

Drawbacks and limitations

The simple design of the Telecaster is part of the guitar's charm, but it does have a few definite shortcomings. The lack of contours on the body necessitates a particular strumming arm position that can be unforgiving; the limited three-saddle bridge design means that intonation is not quite as accurate as it could be, and it has to be said that it's not the most comfortable bridge to rest your right hand upon. In many ways, these limitations informed the next Fender model, the Stratocaster, which had both a finely adjustable bridge and a contoured body.

Chordal punch

The sound of a Fender Telecaster is characterized by a bright, clanging, mid-range tone, with plenty of attack. This 'punch' lends itself to a more percussive style of playing. It has been adapted as the guitar of choice for many country players, the finest and best known of whom has to be Albert Lee.

Rather than the single-note soloing that Strats seem to invite, Telecaster players, such as Keith

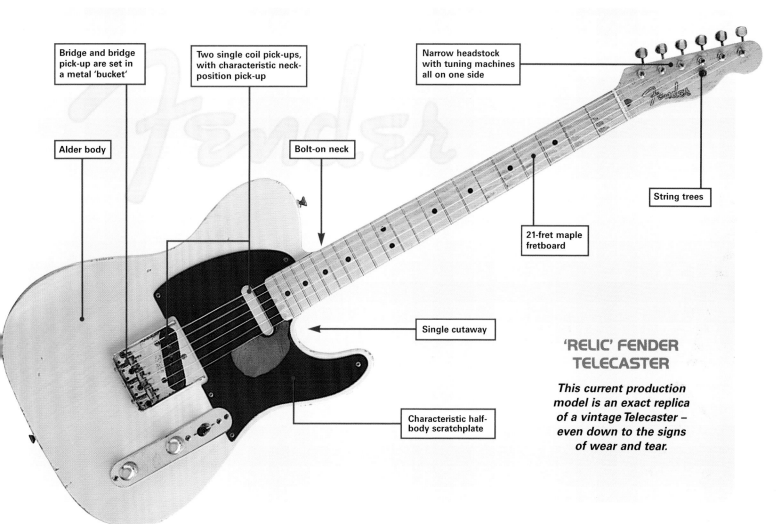

Bridge and bridge pick-up are set in a metal 'bucket'

Two single coil pick-ups, with characteristic neck-position pick-up

Narrow headstock with tuning machines all on one side

Alder body

Bolt-on neck

String trees

21-fret maple fretboard

Single cutaway

'RELIC' FENDER TELECASTER

This current production model is an exact replica of a vintage Telecaster – even down to the signs of wear and tear.

Characteristic half-body scratchplate

Richards, Graham Coxon, Wilko Johnson and Chrissie Hynde, tend to have a chordal style (although, inevitably, there are a few exceptions, such as Bluesman Albert Collins and Jeff Beck).

The simplicity and reliability of Telecasters also seems to invite a fair degree of experimentation – Jonny Greenwood, Will Sergeant (Echo And The Bunnymen), Marc Ribot (a Tom Waits regular) and the Gang Of Four's Andy Gill have all used Telecasters to create new, angular and exciting sounds.

No glamour model

Although there are luxurious sunburst- and paisley-finished Telecasters, the guitars' relatively plain looks are perhaps one reason why they aren't treated with the same degree of reverence as Strats and Les Pauls. However, the basic styling of the 'Fifties and 'Sixties models has its own rugged mystique – it's a workmanlike instrument, more like a trusted tool than a luxury item. The blue-collar, sweat-and-integrity image of the Telecaster chimed perfectly with both Bruce Springsteen, who, at the height of his 'Seventies and 'Eighties success, was invariably seen with a battered Tele, and Joe Strummer of The Clash, who always had one slung over his back like a rifle.

Custom parts and copies

The simplicity of the Tele's design means that there are many copies and versions produced by other companies, and the crudeness of many of its components makes it easy to customize or upgrade with purpose-made parts, such as six-saddle bridges and Humbucker pick-ups. Shechter do a particularly good line of refinements on the Telecaster theme, and these were adopted by many leading players during the 'Eighties, as were Tokai's range of Tele copies.

Three Telecasters, from l to r: Set Neck Junior, American Standard and a reissued 1969 Thinline.

UNDERNEATH THE ARCHES

The story of archtop evolution, and the curvaceous Gretsch 6120.

When Les Paul and Lloyd Loar began experimenting with amplification and pick-ups in the 'Forties, they took the archtop as their starting point. Many design features that are now standard, such as the truss rod, started out as archtop innovations. These guitars, which are also known as cello, orchestra plectrum or f-hole guitars, fall into two categories: electric archtops, which have pick-ups set into the body, and acoustic archtops, which can also have pick-ups attached to the bottom of the neck and suspended above the body.

Construction

The construction of archtops closely resembles that of violins or mandolins. Both the soundboard and back are made from carved or laminated spruce or maple. Unlike flat-tops, archtops need very little internal bracing or bridge reinforcement. This is because the arched shape of the front and back gives the soundbox a great deal of innate strength, and the strings pass over the bridge before being anchored to a tailpiece, which spreads the stress to the rear of the guitar. Archtops have large soundboxes in order to amplify the sound as much as possible. Like their nylon-string cousins, early models had round soundholes, but in the 'Twenties and 'Thirties a vogue emerged for violin-style f-shaped holes.

These Aria archtops resemble the Gibson L-5 and Super 400 models of the 'Thirties.

History

Archtops were first built at the end of the 19th century. As with most innovations in guitar design, their development is bound up in musical trends. In the 'Twenties, jazz big bands were the main musical force in the USA and Europe. In those pre-amplified times, guitarists needed instruments with considerable projection to make themselves heard. The addition of pick-ups allowed pioneers, such as Charlie Christian and Eddie Lang, to take solos. As these solos became ever more adventurous, so the need to have access to the upper end of the guitar's register led to cutaways becoming a standard feature from the 'Fifties onwards.

Manufacturers

Carved-wood, acoustic archtops were the mainstay of the Gibson company's early catalogue. The Style O (1908) and the L-4 (1912) were archtops with round soundholes. The latter was created by Gibson engineer Lloyd Loar, who introduced some important innovations, such as the truss rod and the 'floating' bridge – an adjustable bridge held in place by the tension of the strings. His next 'master model', the L-5, set more trends with its raised fingerboard, f-holes and an internal resonator called a Virzi. Epiphone also made fine archtops (the Emperor and Triumph models), as did Vega, a small company established at the turn of the 19th/20th century, and John D'Angelico, a New York craftsman whose exquisite acoustic archtops are now collectors' items.

Rickenbacker was the first company to go into production with an archtop fitted with a horseshoe magnet pick-up. Its Electro Spanish, or ES, model marked a significant step in the development of the electric guitar. Many companies followed suit, including Gibson, who launched its own ES-150, which became synonymous with Charlie Christian. This guitar was an ancestor of the famous 300 series of the 'Fifties, which combined elements of archtop construction with a new thinline design and a solid centre block for greater sustain.

Golden Gretsch

In the post-war period, most manufacturers launched themselves down the road of solid-body or thinline, semi-acoustic production, but one took a different route.

Brian Setzer (ex-Stray Cats), swinging rock'n'roll virtuoso, playing the Gretsch signature model 6120 that bears his name.

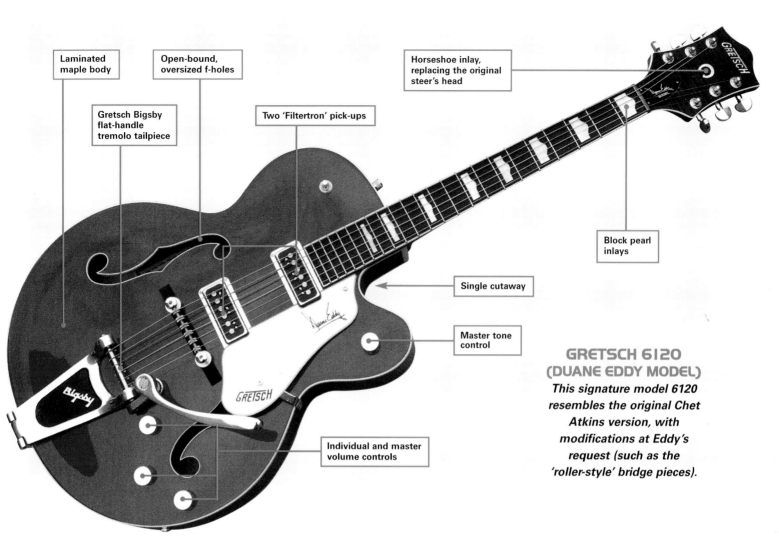

Laminated maple body

Open-bound, oversized f-holes

Horseshoe inlay, replacing the original steer's head

Gretsch Bigsby flat-handle tremolo tailpiece

Two 'Filtertron' pick-ups

Block pearl inlays

Single cutaway

Master tone control

Individual and master volume controls

GRETSCH 6120 (DUANE EDDY MODEL)
This signature model 6120 resembles the original Chet Atkins version, with modifications at Eddy's request (such as the 'roller-style' bridge pieces).

The guitar company of Fred Gretsch, which was already producing archtop acoustics of a reasonable standard, brought out a new electric archtop in the mid-'Fifties with the advice and endorsement of Chet Atkins, one of the most revered and successful instrumentalists of the time, whose style spanned pop, country and jazz.

Gretsch specialized in using laminated rather than carved maple for the bodies of their archtops. The Chet Atkins 6120, launched commercially in 1955, remains the most popular of all Gretsches, sought out by rockabilly, rock'n'roll, jazz and country players for its sound, as well as for its sheer good looks. (Reissued over the next two decades with a variety of different specifications, it was re-christened the Nashville in 1964.) It combined a rich, clear tone with an unmistakable twang, thanks to its Bigsby tailpiece and tremolo. It was adored by rock'n'roll and country players alike, and has been associated with Duane Eddy, Eddie Cochran, Brian Setzer and Chet Atkins himself. Witty and luxurious details, such as fretboard inlays engraved with images of cacti and cows, the head of a longhorn steer inlaid into the headstock (later replaced by a horseshoe) and a Gretsch 'G' branded onto the guitar's body as if it were a prize heifer, all added to its desirability. It became Gretsch's flagship model, closely flanked by the White Falcon, a dazzling white model with gold fittings that was the most expensive guitar you could buy in 1955, and which remains a status symbol – Billy Duffy of The Cult used to brandish one with pride.

Archtops return
Although the company was bought out in 1980, it has since returned to the Gretsch family. To coincide with a resurgence in the popularity of archtops, various versions of the 6120 have been reissued, including the White Falcon and Nashville models. Although they do not have the collectors' value of the originals, they still have the classic twangy Gretsch sound, along with the electronics and hardware of a modern standard.

The extravagant gold-and-white styling of a Gretsch White Falcon.